The Early Austrian School of Economics

This book explores the thought of the three 'founding' members of the Austrian School of economics: Carl Menger, Friedrich von Wieser, and Eugen Böhm-Bawerk, considering the overlapping and specialization of their work on money, value, and capital. Offering an incisive overview of the work of three important, but often-neglected figures, the author sheds fresh light on the transition from Adam Smith's economics and the thought of the German School, to modern economic theory, considering also the influence of the Austrian School on the work of Max Weber. As such, it will appeal to scholars with interests in the history of ideas, economic theory, political economy, and social theory.

Christopher Adair-Toteff is Fellow at the Center for Social and Political Thought, University of South Florida, USA. A philosopher, sociologist, and social theorist, he has published widely in the field of classical sociology. He is the author of *Raymond Aron's Philosophy of Political Responsibility*, *Max Weber's Sociology of Religion*, *Fundamental Concepts in Max Weber's Sociology of Religion*, and *Sociological Beginnings*. He is the editor of *The Anthem Companion to Ernst Troeltsch* and *The Anthem Companion to Ferdinand Tönnies*, and the co-editor of *The Calling of Social Thought: Rediscovering the Work of Edward Shils* and *The Anthem Companion to Raymond Aron*.

T0347548

Routledge Studies in Social and Political Thought

This series explores core issues in political philosophy and social theory. Addressing theoretical subjects of both historical and contemporary relevance, the series has broad appeal across the social sciences. Contributions include new studies of major thinkers, key debates and critical concepts.

The Early Austrian School of Economics
Money, Value, Capital
Christopher Adair-Toteff

The Early Austrian School of Economics
Money, Value, Capital

Christopher Adair-Toteff

Routledge
Taylor & Francis Group

LONDON AND NEW YORK

First published 2022
by Routledge
2 Park Square, Milton Park, Abingdon, Oxon OX14 4RN

and by Routledge
605 Third Avenue, New York, NY 10158

*Routledge is an imprint of the Taylor & Francis Group, an
informa business*

British Library Cataloguing-in-Publication Data
A catalogue record for this book is available from the British
Library

Library of Congress Cataloging-in-Publication Data
Names: Adair-Toteff, Christopher, author.
Title: The early Austrian school of economics : money, value, capital /
Christopher Adair-Toteff.
Description: Abingdon, Oxon ; New York, NY : Routledge, 2022. | Series:
Routledge studies in social and political thought ; volume 1 | Includes
bibliographical references and index.
Identifiers: LCCN 2021061277 | ISBN 9781032045504 (hbk) | ISBN
9781032045511 (pbk) | ISBN 9781003193746 (ebk)
Subjects: LCSH: Austrian school of economics. | Economics.
Classification: LCC HB98 .A37 2022 | DDC 330.15/7--dc23/eng/20220303
LC record available at https://lccn.loc.gov/2021061277

ISBN: 9781032-045504 (hbk)
ISBN: 9781032045511 (pbk)
ISBN: 9781003193746 (ebk)

DOI: 10.4324/9781003193746

Typeset in Times New Roman
by KnowledgeWorks Global Ltd.

Contents

1 The Early Austrian School of Economics

An Introduction

In his posthumously published *Ten Great Economists*, Joseph A. Schumpeter listed Karl Marx and John Maynard Keynes as two of the ten greatest modern economists. Schumpeter also included Alfred Marshall, Marie Esprit Leon Walras, and Vilfredo Pareto in that list of leading economic thinkers. In addition, there are several American and British scholars. Finally, there are three Austrians who Schumpeter also wanted to include in his list of the leading modern economists: Schumpeter himself listed Carl Menger and Eugen von Böhm-Bawerk, while Schumpeter's widow, Elizabeth Brody Schumpeter, added the third—Friedrich von Wieser. Schumpeter clearly recognized that these three scholars were among the very best in the history of modern economics. Not one to bestow honor lightly, Schumpeter regarded Menger as a "born theorist," von Wieser as an "eminent man," and Böhm-Bawerk as nothing less than "the great master" (Schumpeter 1951: 83, 299, 143). Furthermore, Schumpeter knew these three scholars personally, and he held them in high regard. He praised Menger for his single-minded devotion to the young discipline of economics and he lauded Böhm-Bawerk for having served as finance minister in three different administrations and having ensured that Austria's financial condition remained stable under some very difficult circumstances. Furthermore, he agreed with the assessment that von Wieser's incredible knowledge, his penetrating intellect, and his noble personality made him comparable to the great Goethe (Schumpeter 1951: 83, 149, 299). Despite Schumpeter's inclusion of these three Austrians in his list of eminent modern economists, they are largely ignored by historians.[1] There is little doubt that they do not deserve the reputations of Marx or Keynes, but they also do not deserve to be so neglected. Schumpeter reminds us that these three economists were important because they were the founders of the Austrian School of Economics (Schumpeter 1951: 88–89, 142, 298). Today, one is likely to

DOI: 10.4324/9781003193746-1

think of Ludwig von Mises and Friedrich von Hayek as members of the Austrian School of Economics, and one would be correct in doing so. But von Mises and von Hayek were members of the later Austrian School, and it is not certain that the later Austrian School would have come into being, if it were not for Menger, Böhm-Bawerk, and von Wieser. Because it was the three who formed the "österreichische Schule" and it was they who insisted the "field of work of the Austrian economists is theory in the strict sense of the word."[2] Unfortunately, there has been little written about any of these three theorists, and even less on them together. Accordingly, it is the purpose of this book to draw attention to the three founders of the Early Austrian School of Economics. The title of this book is a reflection of their major contributions: Menger for his theory of money, von Wieser for his theory of value, and Böhm-Bawerk for his theory of capital. Schumpeter was not always right or fair, but his high assessment of these three founders of the Early Austrian School of Economics, is both unbiased and correct.[3]

   This Introduction has two additional sections. The first section is devoted to outlining the lives of Menger, von Wieser, and Böhm-Bawerk. Because these three scholars have mostly faded from view, it was suggested that I provide a brief account of their lives. I had considered placing these biographical sketches at the beginning of each chapter, but soon realized that they should be placed together because their lives were so interconnected. The second section is an indication of the goals and limitations of this book, as well as an account of how the main portion of this book is constructed.

Menger, von Wieser, and Böhm-Bawerk

Carl Menger, Friedrich von Wieser, and Eugen von Böhm-Bawerk had much in common: they were Austrians, they were trained in law, and they combined theory with practice. They also knew each other well and they all participated in public life. In his Introduction to his collection of essays on Böhm-Bawerk and von Wieser, Mark Blaug suggested that if Menger was the founder of the Austrian school, then Böhm-Bawerk would be his St. Paul. Von Wieser was also a disciple of Menger's but, unlike Böhm-Bawerk, he mostly refrained from controversy (Blaug 1992: ix–xi). Menger, Böhm-Bawerk, and von Wieser also shared problems regarding their names. It is now rather unusual for a German name to begin with a "C" instead of a "K" but it was not that unusual in the nineteenth century. Thus, there is a fair amount of confusion when some write "Karl Menger" because that was the name of Carl Menger's son. Karl Menger was also an economist but he lived most of his life in England. Whether it is listed in this work as Carl or Karl, it should be understood to refer to Carl the father and not to Karl the son. Friedrich von Wieser's name appears in different forms. It is Friedrich Freiherr von Wieser in many accounts; however, when the Austrian nobility was disbanded in 1919, he was usually referred to as Friedrich Wieser. For this book, the preference is to use the form Friedrich von Wieser. Eugen von Böhm-Bawerk was born Eugen Böhm, but his father was made a noble in 1854. Thus, the name was altered to Eugen Böhn Ritter von Bawerk; he, however, tended to use the form Eugen Böhm-Bawerk or, less frequently, Eugen von Böhm-Bawerk. Böhm-Bawerk will be used throughout.

Carl Menger

Carl Menger was born on February 23, 1840 in Neu-Sandez, which is now part of Poland. His father was an attorney who came from a family of musicians, bureaucrats, and military officers. His mother came from a long line of merchants and had acquired an estate in eastern Austria where Carl spent much of his early years. Both of his younger brothers became relatively famous in their own right: Anton as a professor of economics and a writer on socialism; Max as a member of parliament and also an author of socialist tracts. Carl studied first in Vienna (1859–1860) and then at Prague (1860–1863). Upon graduation, he began to write for a newspaper in Lemberg before moving back to Vienna. It was in his capacity as a journalist that he observed economic conflicts. Subsequently, he moved into government service.

Erich Streissler argued in an extremely informative paper "Carl Menger on economic policy: the lectures to Crown Prince Rudolf" that there was an institutional basis for scholars' lack of sense of Menger's opinions on economic policy. Streissler pointed out that the German universities in the second half of the nineteenth century followed Karl Heinrich Rau's division between theoretical economics and applied economics.[4] That is, there were typically two chairs in economics: one for theory, and one for applied economics. He also noted that this tradition was also followed in Austria, and that Menger's chair was in theory. Streissler argued that the lectures that Menger gave to the Crown Prince during 1876 reveal that Menger was a convinced follower of Adam Smith and a devoted classical liberal. However, he admitted that at the time, there was insufficient proof (Streissler 1990: 110, 119, 129). Whether one agrees with Streissler or not, there is very little evidence that Menger was ever preoccupied with anything but theory.

In his article in *Palgrave's Dictionary of Political Economy*, Friedrich von Wieser devotes a considerable amount of time to defending Menger's early achievement regarding theoretical economics. This was Menger's doctrine of needs, subjective value, prices, and money, which von Wieser insists was the theoretical foundation for the Austrian School of Economics. Von Wieser pointed out that Menger's critics insisted that this theoretical basis was not original to Menger and he noted that no less of an authority than Maffeo Pantaleoni had accused Menger of plagiarizing from Hermann Heinrich Gossen's *Entwicklung der Gesetze des menschlichen Verkehr*. But as von Wieser clarified, Gossen's book was categorically rejected by the German Historical School. As a result, Gossen withdrew the book and it had fallen into "oblivion." It was Jevons who found a copy in the British Museum library and brought it to scholars' attention. Von Wieser continued his defense of Menger, first by noting that Menger had developed his theory independent of Jevons and others and second, by noting that Menger's theory of subjective value went far beyond what Gossen had written (von Wieser 1925c: 924).

The volume that von Wieser was referring to was Menger's *Grundsätze der Volkswirthschaftslehre*. The volume carried a subtitle *Erster, Allgemeiner Theil* but he never published a second part. Von Hayek suggested that Menger had worked feverishly on this book during 1868 and 1869 but it is likely that he was still writing it in 1870. It was published in Vienna in 1871. Von Hayek did note that it was not well received anywhere in Germany, nor did it fare much better in Austria (von Hayek 1968: XVIII). Von Hayek added that Böhm-Bawerk and von Wieser tried to convince more German economists to recognize the book's importance but with little success. In 1876, Menger was invited to become the teacher to the gifted but troubled Crown Prince Rudolf and they spent the next two years traveling through many parts of Europe: England, Scotland, Ireland, France, and Germany. When they finally returned to Austria Menger was appointed to the chair for political economy at Vienna. There he published his other major work *Untersuchungen über die Methode der Sozialwissenschaften und der politischen Ökonomie im besondere*. Unfortunately, this volume was not received much better than his *Grundsätze*; if anything, it provoked a major critical response from Gustav Schmoller and was the beginning of the "battle over methods" known as the "Methodenstreit." Menger concentrated on his teaching, and what he did publish over the next two decades was far less confrontational. He retired in 1903 at the relatively early age of 63 in order to concentrate on writing.[5]

Menger died shortly after his 81st birthday on February 26, 1921. Von Wieser argued for Menger's originality; however, he suggested that Menger never went much further than refining his original thesis. He maintained that it was left to Böhm-Bawerk and himself to develop it. He concluded his article on Menger with the observation that the two major collections, the *Handwörterbuch der Staatswissenschaften* and the *Grundriss der Sozialökonomik*, had the theoretical essays written by Austrians (and not by any Germans) (von Wieser 1925c: 924). Von Wieser was correct in his assertion that the German editors of the two major works turned to the three Austrians to write some major entries on economics. He is probably also correct that Menger's most important work was his *Grundsätze*. Finally, he may have been right that Menger never developed his method, but his writings on money reveal a continuous evolution. Given its prominence in Menger's works and that it was a subject on which he continually revised his ideas, it is the main focus of the chapter discussing him in this book.

Friedrich von Wieser[6]

Friedrich Freiherr von Wieser was born in Vienna on July 10, 1851 to his father Leopold and his mother Mithilde Schulheim von Zandiel. Leopold had served in the Austrian army during the war with Italy and was brought into the ranks of the Austrian nobility in 1859. Friedrich was the fourth of nine children and inherited his artistic talent from his father. Friedrich attended the "Schottengymnasium" and excelled in historical studies. He graduated at the age of 17 and enrolled in the legal program at the university in Vienna. He graduated at the age of 21 with a degree in law. It is noteworthy to remember that his life-long interest was in history, but it becomes even more remarkable when one considers how often the German Historical School criticized von Wieser for his supposed lack of appreciation for historical methods.

After graduating in 1872, von Wieser entered government service, where he would remain for almost a decade. However, he was granted a leave of absence, which allowed him to study in Germany for two years. He studied at Heidelberg, Jena, and Leipzig, with Knies, Roscher, and Hildebrand. He published his first book on the origins of value (*Über den Ursprung und die Hauptgesetze des Wirthschaflichen Werthes*) in 1884 and followed it up in 1889 with *Der natürlichen Werth*. He published numerous essays from then until 1914, when he contributed to Max Weber's *Grundriss der Sozialökonomik* (Adair-Toteff 2021). During these years he taught at Prague from 1884 until 1903. It was in 1903 that von Wieser was appointed to Menger's chair and with a one year's absence toward the end of the war, he remained there until his retirement in 1923. His final work was similar to his earlier work for Weber and it emphasized the sociological aspects of economics. This was *Das Gesetz der Macht (The Law of Power)*, which appeared in 1926. Blaug suggested that it was von Wieser's interest in the connection between economics and sociology that hindered his acceptance by fellow economists. Blaug also maintained that von Wieser's concern with the rational foundations of natural value suggested that socialist countries could also have rational economies and that von Wieser's theory of value was the target of Ludwig von Mises' argument that socialism was antithetical to rational economic calculations (Blaug 1992: xi). While Blaug contended that von Wieser's reputation never matched those of Menger or Böhm-Bawerk, he observed that von Wieser attracted more Austrian students than either of his more famous colleagues (Blaug 1992: xi–xii).

Von Wieser had suffered from ill health in his final year and was battling a lung infection in July of 1926. It seemed that he was slowly recovering when he took a turn for the worse. He died at his summer home in Brunnwinkel, which is in the Salzkammergut not too far from Salzburg. He had just finished his article on "Geld" for the fourth edition of the *Handwörterbuch der Staatswissenschaften* and had celebrated his seventy-fifth birthday just two weeks previously. It is an indication of his importance that the editors of the *Handwörterbuch* inserted a notice of his death in the opening pages of the volume that contained his essay on "Geld."

Friedrich von Wieser was trained as a lawyer but became a national economist and toward the end of his life was primarily a social economist. As such, his preoccupation with "value" ("Wert") also changed over time. Whereas it was of little concern to him during his student years pursuing his legal degree, it became the focal point of his academic work for the rest of his life. In the 1880s and 1890s, he was intent upon providing a scholarly account of value, but for the remaining 25 years, he was more interested in how "value" impacted peoples' lives. In light of this, it is not surprising to note that von Wieser's ideas about the relationship between social interaction and economics has some similarities with those of Max Weber. These similarities, and their differences, will be briefly discussed in this book's "Epilogue." While there are some, like Mark Blaug, who thought that von Wieser's influence paled against the originality of Menger and the combativeness of Böhm-Bawerk, I suggest that his influence was just as extensive as that of his fellow Austrians. In his "Friedrich Freiherr von Wieser" Friedrich von Hayek noted that with his death, the world had not only lost a great teacher and a great national economist, but that Austria had lost a great statesman and a great patriot (von Hayek 1929: V).

Eugen Böhm-Bawerk

Eugen Böhm-Bawerk was born on February 12, 1851 in Brünn (Brno), which is now part of the Czech Republic. His father died while Böhm-Bawerk was young and the family moved to Vienna (Weiss 1924: III). He attended the "Schottengymnasium" ("Scottish Gymnasium") at the same time as Friedrich von Wieser. It was at that school that they began a friendship that lasted until Böhm-Bawerk's death. In his account in *Palgrave's Dictionary of Political Economy*, von Wieser noted how strong and long lasting that friendship was (Wieser 1925b: 825). After graduating from the university at Vienna in 1872, Böhm-Bawerk joined the Austrian Ministry of Finance and while there, earned his doctorate in law in 1875. He was then supported with the Ministry's money in order to spend two years studying in Germany. He studied with Karl Knies at Heidelberg, Wilhelm Roscher at Jena, and Bruno Hildebrand at Leipzig. The fact that he was asked to participate in the 1896 "Festschrift" for Knies is sufficient indication of the regard that Knies and other Germans had for Böhm-Bawerk. In 1880 Böhm-Bawerk qualified as a "Privatdozent" in political economy at Vienna and became an "Extraordinarious" professor. The following year he moved to the university at Innsbruck and became an "Ordinarious" professor there in 1884. He remained at Innsbruck until 1889 when he returned to Vienna and back into government service. He was initially appointed as an advisor but was soon promoted to "section chief" in charge of major taxation reform. In 1895 Böhm-Bawerk became Minister of Finance for the first of three times. The first time was rather brief, while the second period lasted from November 1897 to March 1898. The third period was the longest, from 1900 until 1904. In 1899, Böhm-Bawerk was made a member of the upper house where he was regarded by almost everyone as a fighter. However, they also regarded him as one who was unfailingly fair and always acted with dignity regarding his opponents as well as his supporters. Von Wieser wrote that Böhm-Bawerk's political tact and good judgment allowed him to be far more successful than anyone before him. And, he remained in government service during those intervals when he was no longer finance minister (Von Wieser 1925b: 825). In 1904, Böhm-Bawerk left his ministerial position for the final time and returned to teaching at the university in Vienna, where he would remain until his death. Böhm-Bawerk died unexpectedly on August 27, 1914 while on vacation in Kramsach, Tirol, Austria. Böhm-Bawerk left behind his wife but no children. In 1880, he had married Paula von Wieser, the sister of his close friend Friedrich von Wieser. Böhm-Bawerk is best remembered for his book on capital. *Kapital und Kapitalzins* was first published in two volumes with the first, more critical volume appearing in 1884, and the second, and more constructive, volume appearing in 1889. It then appeared in a second edition in 1900, and then a third edition in 1912. This edition of *Kapital und Kapitalzins* was expanded from the earlier editions and appeared in three volumes. It was his theory of capital that secured his place among the leading modern economists (Zwiedineck-Südenhorst, O. von. 1955: 385–386).

Friedrich von Wieser praised his friend for his ability to combine analytical criticism with positive theory, especially with regard to his theory of capitalism and interest (Von Wieser 1925b: 826). Carl Menger praised Böhm-Bawerk for his governmental service, his dedication to teaching, but above all, for his brilliant and ground-breaking scholarly work (Menger 1970: 303–304, 307). But Böhm-Bawerk was also instrumental in the establishment and the maintenance of the *Zeitschrift für Volkswirtschaft, Sozialpolitik und Verwaltung.* Founded in 1892, it soon became Austria's leading economic journal. In his moving tribute to his co-editor, Eugen von Philippovich acknowledged the major role that Böhm-Bawerk played in that journal and reminded his readers that Böhm-Bawerk's final essay "Macht und ökonomisches Gesetz" appeared in the same issue as Philippovich's obituary (Philippovich 1914: 444). But it was Joseph Schumpeter who pointed out in 1915 that Böhm-Bawerk's death was too recent and his presence still too powerful to allow an objective account of the man and his work. Nonetheless, Schumpeter published a sixty-plus page essay on his teacher in German (Schumpeter 1914). What is included in *Ten Great Economists* is an abbreviated translation of that work (Schumpeter 1951: 143, note). Schumpeter admitted proudly that he was a disciple of Böhm-Bawerk and was personally devoted to him. But he was objective enough to recognize the enormity of his master's achievements. That Böhm-Bawerk was able to build upon Menger's theory of economic progress was enough to secure his place as "one of the five or six great economists of all time," accomplishment enough (Schumpeter 1951: 147). But, until Böhm-Bawerk, only Marx had recognized that capitalism was fundamentally based upon interest and profit, and that "Marx's system is in its core nothing but a theory of interest and profit" (Schumpeter 1951: 147). Franz Weiss maintained that this work was the best critique of Marx's theory of value (Weiss 1924: VIII). In Schumpeter's opinion, Böhm-Bawerk was a theorist, a pioneer, and an architect (Schumpeter 1951: 146, 159). Toward the conclusion of his essay on his master, Schumpeter wrote: "To say that his work is immortal is to express a triviality." (Schumpeter 1951: 189).

Weiss insisted that Böhm-Bawerk was never concerned with fame and always focused on his work (Weiss 1924: XIII–XV). Although both von Wieser and Böhm-Bawerk are often regarded as followers of Carl Menger, their writings prove that they were their "master's" equals and that all three were founders of the Early School of Austrian economics.

Goals, Limitations, and Structure

The purpose of this book is to offer a clear and unbiased appraisal of the theories of these three thinkers, first by providing a general overview of each of their writings and then by focusing on each of their most notable contributions. In Menger's case the contribution is on money; in von Wieser's case it is on value; and for Böhm-Bawerk it is on capital. Because they were members of the same school means that they tended to share the same ideas and approaches. However, they were not always in agreement, so I will also discuss their disagreements. Just because von Wieser and Böhm-Bawerk were Menger's pupils should not be taken to mean that they always agreed with their master. Nor should the fact that von Wieser and Böhm-Bawerk were brothers-in-law lead one to believe that they completely shared their ideas. I will also refrain from taking sides in any discussion of Menger and Schmoller in the "Methodenstreit." Unlike Max Alter, who seemed to prefer Schmoller and the Younger German Historical School to Menger and the Early Austrian School, I prefer not to take sides (see Alter 1990; White 1990: 356–357). Instead, I recognize and appreciate the strengths and the weaknesses of both sides. In addition, I acknowledge the enormous challenges facing anyone who wishes to tackle these theories because they were written at the end of the nineteenth century and at the beginning of the twentieth in the academic German of the time. In line with this, I follow Lawrence H. White's admonition to use "terms as plain and unsubtle as possible" (White 1990: 349). My goal is to explain what these three scholars believed in terms of economic theory and what they meant by money, value, and capital. That means that I mostly forgo considering how these thinkers responded to their contemporaries outside of Austria. Finally, I acknowledge that this book is no more than an introduction, written by a scholar who is not an economist by training. Whether professional economists will find much of interest will be up to them; the focus here is on the *socio* aspects of socio-economics. In this, I am emphasizing a side of Austrian economics that has always been misunderstood. In his 1914 tribute to Böhm-Bawerk, Philippovich defended him from the charge that Böhm-Bawerk was only interested in theory. Philippovich argued that, like Menger and von Wieser, Böhm-Bawerk was also concerned with practical social problems (Philippovich 1914: 441–442). Apart from this chapter, this book has four additional chapters. Chapter 2 discusses Carl Menger and has two major sections. The first section is devoted to Carl Menger's economic theory as set out in several of his books and some of his articles. The second section concentrates on his conceptions of *money* as he conceived it in his three editions of his article "Geld" and in related articles. Chapter 3 is devoted to Friedrich von Wieser and also has two major sections. The first is devoted to von Wieser's general conception of economics as he formulated it in various minor and major writings. The second concentrates on his notions regarding *value* as he set it out in his two books from the 1880s and from later articles. Chapter 4 is focused on Eugen von Böhm-Bawerk and, as with the previous chapters, it also has two major sections. The first is a discussion of Eugen von Böhm-Bawerk's economic theories as reflected in a number of articles. The second is concentrated on his notion of *capital* as he examined it and related economic ideas in his multi-volume work that first appeared in the 1880s. Chapter 5 is a brief concluding chapter and takes up four issues: First, it is a brief summary of the main points that were developed in the three central chapters. Second, it is a brief response to a number of criticisms leveled against the three Austrians. Third, it is a very limited attempt to indicate Max Weber's assessment of the Austrians compared to the members of the German Historical School. Fourth, and finally, it is my answer to the question of why read the works of the members of the Early Austrian School of Economics. The first chapter was prospective and the fifth chapter mostly a look back, but the three main chapters provide an account of the Early Austrians' theories of *money, value, and capital*, hence, the title of this book. It is hoped that this book will help stimulate others to take a closer look at the theoretical writings of these three vital members of the Early Austrian School of Economics.

Notes

1 A partial exception is Mark Blaug's *Eugen von Böhm-Bawerk (1851–1914) and Friedrich von Wieser (1851–1926)* but despite the title, it is not a work on them. Rather, it is a collection of 15 articles published between 1888 and 1988. While these articles are all valuable and will be referred to, they mostly omit discussions of Carl Menger. Blaug 1992.
2 "Das Arbeitsfeld der österrichische Schule ist die Theorie im strengen Sinne des Wortes." Böhm-Bawerk (1924). 205. Wieser 1925a

3 Schumpeter's opinion of the three remained largely unchanged throughout much of his life. His essay on Böhm-Bawerk was originally published in 1914; his appraisal of Menger appeared in 1921; and his appreciation of von Wieser appeared in English in 1927.

4 Streissler clarified that Rau had three divisions: theory, applied, and public finance but that the last one tended to be rotated between the two professors. Streissler 1990: 107.

5 In his "Einleitung" to Menger's *Gesammelte Schriften,* Friedrich von Hayek also noted that Menger, Jevons, and Walras had independently arrived at the principle of marginal utility. Von Hayek 1968: VII. It is worth indicating that there are two collections of essays on Menger— both stemmed from conferences. These papers are found in Hicks and Weber 1973 and in Caldwell 1990a. The best accounts of Menger's life are still those by von Wieser and von Hayek.

6 Because von Wieser had outlived Böhm-Bawerk and Menger, there are no contemporary accounts about von Wieser from either of them. The two best discussions of von Wieser are von Hayek's account in von Wieser's *Gesammelte Abhandlungen* and von Wieser's address in honor of the one hundredth anniversary of the Scottish Gymnasium ("Schottengymnasium") that he gave in 1907. See von Wieser 1929a. 335–345.

References

Adair-Toteff, C. (2021) *Max Weber and the Path from Political Economist to Social Economist*. Abingdon: Routledge.

Alter, M. (1990) "What do we know about Menger?" In *Carl Menger and His Legacy in Economics*. Annual Supplement to Volume 22, History of Political Economy. Durham and London: Duke University Press. 313–348.

Blaug, M., (ed.) (1992) *Eugen von Böhm-Bawerk (1851–1914) and Friedrich von Wieser (1851–1926)*. Aldershot: Edward Elgar Publishing Limited.

Böhm-Bawerk, E. von (1924) "Die österreichische Schule." In *Gesammelte Schriften*. Herausgegeben von Franz X. Weiss. Frankfurt a. Main: Verlag Sauer & Auvermann. 205–229.

Caldwell, B.J., (ed.) (1990a) *Carl Menger and His Legacy in Economics*. Annual Supplement to Volume 22, History of Political Economy. Durham and London: Duke University Press.

Caldwell, B.J. (1990b) "Editor's Introduction." In Caldwell B.J. (ed.), *Carl Menger and His Legacy in Economics*. Annual Supplement to Volume 22, History of Political Economy. Durham and London: Duke University Press. 3–14.

Hayek, F.A. (1929) "Friedrich Freiherr von Wieser." In *Gesammelte Abhandlungen. Mit einer biographischen Einleitung*. Herausgegeben von Friedrich A. v. Hayek. Tübingen: Verlag von J.C.B. Mohr (Paul Siebeck). V–XXIX.

Hayek, F. A. (1968)(1934) "Einleitung." In *Gesammelte Schriften*. Herausgegeben mit einer Einleitung und einem Schriftenverzeichnis von F.S. Hayek. Tübingen: J.C.B. Mohr (Paul Siebeck). 2. Auflage. Band I. VII–XXXVI.

Hicks, J.R. and Weber, W., (eds.). (1973) *Carl Menger and the Austrian School of Economics*. Oxford: Clarendon Press.

Menger, C. (1970) *Gesammelte Schriften*. Herausgegeben mit einer Einleitung und einem Schriftenverzeichnis von F.S. Hayek. Tübingen: J.C.B. Mohr (Paul Siebeck). 2. Auflage. Band III.

Philippovich, E. von (1914) "Eugen von Böhm-Bawerk." *Zeitschrift für Volkswirtschaft, Sozialpolitik und Verwaltung*. Band 23. 439–453.

Schumpeter, J.A. (1914) "Das wissenschaftliche Lebenswerk Eugen von Böhm-Bawerk." *Zeitschrift für Volkswirtschaft, Sozialpolitik und Verwaltung*. Band 23. 454–528.

Schumpeter, J. A. (1951) *Ten Great Economists. From Marx to Keynes*. New York: Oxford University Press.

Streissler, E.W. (1990) "Carl Menger on economic policy: the lectures to Crown Prince Rudolf." In Caldwell B.J. (ed.), *Carl Menger and His Legacy in Economics*. Annual Supplement to Volume 22, History of Political Economy. Durham and London: Duke University Press. 107–130.

Weiss, F.X. (1924) "Eugen von Böhm-Bawerk." In *Gesammelte Schriften*. Herausgegeben von Franz X. Weiss. Frankfurt a. Main: Verlag Sauer & Auvermann. Band I. V–XV.

White, L. H. (1990) "Restoring an 'Altered' Menger." In Caldwell B.J. (ed.), *Carl Menger and His Legacy in Economics*. Annual Supplement to Volume 22, History of Political Economy. Durham and London: Duke University Press. 349–358.

Wieser, F. (1925a) "Austrian School of Economists." In Higgens H. (ed.), *Palgrave's Dictionary of Political Economy*. Vol. 1 A–E. London: Macmillan and Co. 814–818.

Wieser, F. (1925b) "Böhm-Bawerk, Eugen von." In Higgens H. (ed.), *Palgrave's Dictionary of Political Economy*. Vol. 1 A–E. London: Macmillan and Co. 825–826.

Wieser, F. (1925c) "Menger, Carl." In Higgens H. (ed.), *Palgrave's Dictionary of Political Economy*. Vol. II. F–M. London: Macmillan and Co. 923–924.

Wieser, F. von (1929a) *Gesammelte Abhandlungen. Mit einer biographischen Einleitung*. Herausgegeben von Friedrich A. v. Hayek. Tübingen: Verlag von J.C.B. Mohr (Paul Siebeck).

Wieser, F. von (1929b) "Karl Menger." (sic). In *Gesammelte Abhandlungen. Mit einer biographischen Einleitung*. Herausgegeben von Friedrich A. v. Hayek. Tübingen: Verlag von J.C.B. Mohr (Paul Siebeck). 110–125.

Zwiedineck-Südenhorst, O. von (1955) "Böhm-Bawerk (Böhm v. Bawerk), Eugen Ritter v." In *Neue deutsche Biographie*. Herausgegeben von Otto zu Stolberg-Wernigerode. Berlin. Bd. 2: Behaim-Bürkel. 385–386.

2 Menger and Money

Carl Menger

In 1891, Carl Menger wrote a rather brief but crucially important article on the relationship between classical national economy and modern economic politics. However, the title "Die Social-Theorien der classischen National-Oekonomie und der moderne Wirtschaftspolitk" obscures the fact that Menger's work is not really an economic sketch; instead, it is actually a powerful defense of Adam Smith. Written for the centennial of Smith's death, it can also be regarded as an autobiographical account. Menger refers to the account that Babeuf had given before being beheaded: it was not death he feared, but that the account of his work would be written by his opponents.[1] Menger's point was that in Germany it has been Smith's opponents who have written the history of Smith's economics, and they have painted a picture of him as champion of the rich and a proponent of laissez-faire. Moreover, they have represented him in a negative light in German economic histories as being "kapitalistisch, abstrakt, volksfeindlich" (Menger 1970d: 220) (Menger 1970c). These complaints of being capitalistic, abstract, and an enemy of the people are really the same complaints that Menger's German opponents had been leveling at him. They had insisted that Menger's economic theories were too abstract and that he was indifferent to the plight of the worker. They also suggested that he sided with the capitalists and believed in laissez-faire individualistic economics.[2] But Menger argued that the German criticisms applied only to Manchester economics and not to Smith's classical economics. Menger also argued that while Smith did write about wealth and capitalism, he also championed workers' rights and he fought for better working conditions (Menger 1970d: 223, 229–230). In Menger's opinion, the German "new social-political school" may have fought and overcome the members of the "capitalistic Manchesterism" but they have not repudiated Adam Smith and the classical national economy. What they had done was simply to misrepresent what Adam Smith

DOI: 10.4324/9781003193746-2

really believed and actually wrote. In fact, Smith's opponents promoted "misunderstandings and misattributions" ("Missverständnisse und Missdeutungen"), which go against the duty that one has to "objective science" ("objektiven Wissenschaft") (Menger 1970d: 233). In the second section of his essay Menger tries to correct that picture of Adam Smith. He notes that both Smith's classical school and the modern social political school recognize that the working class is economically disadvantaged. The difference is that the earlier school wanted to correct this by reducing the state's interference, whereas the modern school contended that the state should involve itself further in determining economic policy (Menger 1970d: 234–236, 244). Menger's larger point was that the modern school believed itself to be the opponent of the classical school and sought to write the history of its opponents. Menger sought to correct it. Menger's invocation of Babeuf's fear that the history of his work would be written by his opponents was aimed primarily at the German Historical School's misleading account of Smith's economic philosophy, but it was not the only target.

Carl Menger's economic philosophy has often been rewritten by his opponents—either from the members of the German Historical School, and in particular, Gustav Schmoller, or Menger's successors in the Austrian School, in particular, by the older Schumpeter. This chapter on Menger is intended to challenge those portraits. It is designed to present an accurate account of Menger's economic philosophy in general and one devoted to his theory of money in particular.[3]

Menger's Works

Carl Menger is usually regarded as an opponent of the German Historical School but his opposition is less than is often thought. Instead, there is a respectful approach which is amply indicated in Menger's first work *Grundsätze der Volkswirthschaftslehre*. It was published in 1871 by Wilhelm Braumüller in Vienna.[4] Its title indicates that it is about the principles of economic theory. While "Lehre" is often justifiably translated as "doctrine" or "teaching," Menger's employment here makes it clear that he does mean "theory." This is also indicated by the fact that he begins three sections with the term "essence" ("Wesen").[5] And, it is Menger's insistence on the fundamental importance of theory that is usually considered to be the basis of his opposition to the German Historical School. However, there are two things in the early pages of this book which should be taken as an indication of Menger's respect for the German Historical School: first, that Menger dedicates his book to Dr. Wilhelm Roscher "in respectful honor" ("In Achtungsvoller Verehrung") and second, that he is sending this book as a "friendly greeting from a similar-minded thinker from Austria."[6] If one objects that Menger wrote this before the "Methodenstreit" and that his opinion became negative after that, one only needs to read Menger's 1894 essay "Wilhelm Roscher."[7] There, Menger referred to Roscher as the "Nestor" of the German national-economics and the revered leader of the Historical School of German economics. Menger noted that there were other German scholars who emphasized the importance of history in scholarship, but it was Roscher, more than anyone else, who insisted that it was key to understanding economics and solving social-political problems. However, Menger noted that Roscher had never provided a complete methodological program and that contributed to the misunderstanding of the differences between the German Historical School and the Austrian School of Economics. Thus, it was easy for critics to oversimply their opponents' respective positions—that the Germans believed in deduction and the Austrians in induction. Yet both schools insisted on the critical need for empirical data; therefore, the real difference between the two schools was that the Germans emphasized the importance of facts and the Austrians insisted on the need for theories to explain those facts. Both schools acknowledged the scientific need for laws; they just differed on the type of economic "laws." Regardless of the differences, although Roscher's fame was recognized throughout the world, Menger insisted that his contributions were not recognized as much as by those in the Austrian School (Menger 1970a: 273–275, 279–281).

Now we return to the book that provided the theoretical foundations for the Early Austrian School of economics—Menger's *Grundsätze*. The first chapter suggests that Menger believes in universal laws and general objectivity. The chapter title is "The General Theory of Goods" ("Die Allgemeine Lehre vom Gute"), and he introduces the topic by making the assertion that all things are governed by the universal law of causality. He underscores this by referring to Aristotle, who also wrote about the imperative to satisfy human needs. However, Menger moves immediately to qualify this by making four presuppositions. First, a human need; second, a particular thing which can satisfy that human need; third, the knowledge that that thing can causally satisfy that human need; fourth, the availability of that thing which can satisfy that human need (Menger 1968b: 1–3). He also maintains that only in instances in which all four apply can a thing be regarded as a "good" ("Gute") and that if these four presuppositions do not apply, then the thing will simply remain a thing and not a "good." Menger quickly turns from that sense of universality and objectivity to subjectivity—that these four presuppositions demonstrate that the quality of good does not reside in the object, but is simply an indication of our own subjective need (Menger 1968b: 3, footnote). Once again, Menger refers to Aristotle who distinguished between "true" and "illusionary" goods, and maintained that only the former can satisfy human needs. In addition, Menger suggests that Aristotle recognized only basic goods because it is only with the growth of a "higher culture" does the need for "true" goods expand. It is important to point out that Menger is not making a value judgment about lower and higher cultures, but an economic point about the differences in quantity and quality between lower and higher cultures (Menger 1968b: 4 and footnote). Similarly, he is making an economic point when he repeats his claim that the quality of a good is not inherent in some object but in our recognition that that object can satisfy our need (Menger 1968b: 7).

Menger is careful to make sure that this observation is not interpreted to be an assertion that human needs and the things which can satisfy them are not to be regarded as being individual and capricious. Rather, he reminds us that human needs and those goods which can satisfy them stand under the law of causation just like all other things. The bread that we eat, the flour that it is made from, the grain that provides the basis for the flour, and the field in which the grain is grown—these are all "goods." And each of these is also governed by causality (Menger 1968b: 7). However, Menger adds that it is not sufficient that a thing be "good"; the quality that "good" is, is also important. That is to say that the higher the "good's quality" ("Güterqualität"), the better the chance that it will satisfy the human need (Menger 1968b: 18).

Menger now makes another startling assertion; namely, that time is just as an important factor in economics as the law of causality. Menger arrives at this conclusion on the basis of the fact that economics does not deal with a static situation, but is a process in which "goods" are rated more or less valuable depending upon the individual's current need for them. And, he reminds us that the law of causality is not atemporal but it closely bound to the idea of time ("Zeit") (Menger 1968b: 21). He explains that this is a process, with a beginning and a becoming; thus, it is only thinkable in terms of time. As this is a causal process, the length of time varies from case to case. This means that there is considerable uncertainty, both in terms of quantity and quality (Menger 1968b: 21–24). Menger points to how the differences in soil type, its degree of saltiness, and the various types of manure, impact the rate of plant growth. He also points to how the changes in weather affect the growth and even the life of the plant. Menger insisted that economic uncertainty is one of the most consequential factors and has the greatest impact on human economics (Menger 1968b: 26).

Rather than regarding uncertainty as a constant problem, Menger argues that throughout history humans have progressed in ways to minimize the degree of uncertainty. Instead of concentrating on the most basic goods, humans have expanded their desires and needs for higher order goods. That meant transitioning from a rather limited exchange with a few local people to a much larger process of exchange with many people from different places (Menger 1968b: 28–31, 38–39). But Menger continues to insist on the importance of time—that is, the foreseeable future. It is not simply a matter of satisfying one's basic and immediate needs; one must consider future needs and make plans for satisfying them (Menger 1968b: 44–46). This also means trying to determine how many workers are needed, how much material they will need, and how much time they will need to produce those goods. It also means trying to determine who will purchase these goods and the means of transportation needed to convey the product to the buyer (Menger 1968b: 46–47).

Menger next turns to the question of supply and demand and offers three scenarios: 1) the demand is greater than the supply, 2) the demand is less than the supply, and 3) the supply is equal to the demand (Menger 1968b: 51). In both case number 2 and in number 3, there is no real need for economics because the number of goods is equal to or larger than the demand for them. It is only in case number 1 where there is need for economics, which is really planning for how to satisfy future needs (Menger 1968b: 52–55). He also discusses how these needs change, and he offers an illustration of a mountain village and its stream. Normally, the villagers require 200,000 pails of water, but there are times when massive rainfall or melting snow produces 300,000 pails of water. In this case, there is a surplus of 100,000 pails of water. But Menger also conceives of a time in which there is a massive drought and the stream produces only 100,000 pails, leaving a deficit of 100,000 pails of water. In the first two cases, the villagers do not need to be concerned about water because the water supply is equal to or greater than their needs. It is only in the third case where they need to be concerned—it is then that their water needs cannot be met and the supply must be considered economically (Menger 1968b: 57–59). His point is that not all "goods" are "economic goods" (Menger 1968b: 61). Since "economic goods" are scarce goods, the issue becomes one of ownership; i.e., "property."[8] Menger is not interested in property for its own sake, but rather for what it actually has in terms of value.

Value ("Werth") is not only the topic of the lengthiest chapter of the book (chapter 3, 75 pages) but is also key to its understanding.

Chapter 3 is entitled "The Theory of Value" ("Die Lehre von Werthe") and has three sections: the first one is rather brief at ten pages, while the third one has twenty pages and the second one is the largest at thirty-six pages. The first section uses many of the terms and concepts from the previous two chapters. These include the concept of "need," the "notion of "goods," and the definition of economics. He also repeats his concept of economic "goods." In addition, he begins to lay out his argument against the prevailing conception of value; that is, the concept that value is an objective one and is indifferent to human evaluation. Menger was aware of the radical nature of his idea that value was subjective and that is why he begins his chapter on value by noting the importance of the "value of goods" ("Güterwerth") (Menger 1968b: 77). He again stresses that only those goods that we need have economic value; indeed, those things that we have no need for have no value. He again provides two illustrations of the idea of objects which lack value. Someone living in an immense forest has use for only a few trees. These have value for him, but the other hundreds do not. Similarly, someone living next to a large stream can make use of only a few buckets of water per day; thus, most of the water rushes away and has no use and consequently no value (Menger 1968b: 78–84). Menger then states that there is another step—the person needs to know that he needs that object. As he puts it, we need to recognize the usefulness and to know that the object in question is one that can satisfy our need. He insists that value does not reside in the object itself nor is it an inherent property of the thing itself. Rather, it is the realization that the object is something that can satisfy one's need. Hence, Menger's theory of value is subjective.[9]

The second section is "On the Most Original Standard of the Value of Goods" ("Ueber das ursprünglichste Mass des Güterwerthes"). The beginning of this chapter lays out the case that even though objects have economic value if we recognize that they can satisfy needs, not all needs are equal. The purpose of this section is to investigate how we recognize the varying degrees of importance. He suggests that this is a two-step process. First, how much does the satisfaction of a concrete need mean to the individual? This is a personal question so Menger regards it as a "subjective moment." Second, how much does that particular good actually satisfy the individual's specific need? This is not a personal matter but can be independently determined. Hence, Menger regards this as an "objective moment." (Menger 1968b: 87–88). The conclusion is that a satisfaction of a need is both a subjective claim as well as an objective observation and as such, the "good" has a varying degree of worth. Menger spends the next twenty-five pages explaining the difference between the subjective moment and the objective one. As much as his critics accused Menger of emphasizing psychology, he spends most of his effort in discussing how needs are actually met. He uses questions about how much water will satisfy an individual and how much gold will satisfy the same person. This leads to that issue regarding the value of an object and the claim that the rarer it is, the more value it has. As Menger points out, without water the person will perish whereas he can live quite well without gold or diamonds (Menger 1968b: 113–114). This leads Menger to explore how the difference in quality can influence the value of a "good." He uses two examples: wood from a pine tree and food. While the quality of the pine tree may be important to some people, the quality of the food will be crucial to all. He clarifies this by discussing the amount of heat that the pine can generate in contrast to other types of wood that give off longer lasting heat (Menger 1968b: 115–116). As another example, Menger refers to how the qualitative differences in grain will influence how a farmer will determine the grain's use. The poorest will be used for only storage, the middle quality will be used for animal feed, and the best quality will be used for human consumption (Menger 1968b: 117–118).

Menger points out that in discussing the value of the good, it does not reside in the object itself. Thus, it is erroneous to discuss an objective "essence" ("Wesen") of a good; rather, it is a matter of the subjective "measure" ("Mass") of the object. In addition, it will be a variation determined by different individuals. But Menger's more important point is that it is the individual who determines the value of something and that the value does not reside independently from the individual. That is why he devotes the final section of this chapter to discrediting a number of claims that the value resides outside of the individual, namely 1) value is actually determined by the land and location in which the object is found; 2) value is determined by the means of production; 3) value is determined by the worker's labor; 4) value is determined by how much the buyer thinks the product is worth (Menger 1968b: 127, 130, 144, 147, 151–152). As Menger insists, it is the subjective valuation which determines the value of a thing; the "economizing" individual is the most important factor in determining something's price (Menger 1968b: 135).

There are five more chapters in Menger's *Grundsätze*, and chapters 4 to 7 will be discussed here while chapter 8 will be examined in the next part because it is devoted to the concept of money. The four chapters are rather brief and are devoted primarily to the limitations of exchange, thereby leading to the need for money.

Chapter 4 is "The Theory of Exchange" ("Die Lehre vom Tausche") and Menger notes that it is in human nature that there is a need and a desire for exchange. Thus, exchange is not only a matter of necessity but is a matter of enjoyment (Menger 1968b: 153–155). This leads Menger to the observation that not every exchange is an economic one; it is economical only if there is a general need to exchange things in order to satisfy a genuine physical need. In other words, two people must exchange things that they do not need for things that they do need. Both people assign value to those things to be exchanged (Menger 1968b: 158–160. The second section of this chapter focuses on the limitations of economic exchange ("Die Grenzen des ökonomischen Tausches"). Menger spends a fair amount of time discussing the possible exchanges between two people. One has horses while the other has cows; and each has more than they need. Hence, they want to exchange their surplus animals for the ones that they lack. Menger goes into considerable detail of the various possibilities (Menger 1968b: 163–167). What he draws from these examples are the limits of exchange. First, there is the limited time frame. Since the two people have immediate needs and they can only do the exchange in person, they must arrange to meet as soon as is possible. Second, there is the quantity involved. Because of the constraints of time and the need for personal involvement, the number of animals that can be exchanged is somewhat limited. Third, and perhaps most important, is the value that each person gives to his animal, but also the value that he assigns to the other person's animal (Menger 1968b: 167–168). As a related observation, Menger maintains that as the process of exchange begins to expand to include some others, the rate of value is subject to greater variation. This variation can fluctuate to such a degree that rather than there being two people who "win" in the exchange, there is someone who ends up with a rather bad bargain. This individual is what Menger calls "the economic victim" ("die ökonomischen Opfer") (Menger 1968b: 169–170).

Chapters 4, 5, 6, and 7 are brief discussions about exchange, price, and goods. As with much of this book, Menger takes aim at both scholarly and popular misconceptions about these topics. There are several important points that Menger makes in these chapters. First, an economist may want to think of economic issues in the abstract but it is better to provide concrete illustrations. Second, both with exchange and sales, there are at least two individuals involved in these transactions. Third, the value of something changes over time, regardless whether there is an exchange or a sale. Fourth, the desire for a particular exchange or sale will be dependent on the individual's perceived need for the object of exchange or sale and that perceived need may

alter over time (Menger 1968b: 173, 181, 192, 213, 234–235, 247–249).
Menger's *Grundsätze* contains a wealth of great economic ideas but
among the most challenging are his comments about subjective evaluation and how time impacts economic transactions of any type.
The lapse of time between Menger's first book and his second one
was twelve years, and as T.W. Hutchison pointed out the later book
is "a very different kind."[10] Hutchison noted that the *Grundsätze*
had a classic quality but the *Untersuchungen über die Methode der
Socialwissenschaften und der politischen Ökonomie Insbesondere* is
focused on the dispute regarding methods (Hutchison 1973: 15). But
he also noted that Menger was not just critical of Schmoller and the
German Historical School, he was highly critical of Smith and his followers. And he also noted that some observers contended that Menger's
quarrel was with Schmoller and the "younger" Historical School,
but Hutchison suggested that Menger's claim about the lack of clarity applied both to the "younger" and the "older" School (Hutchison
1973: 33). That is because Menger contended that both schools relied
on the German school of historical jurisprudence (Menger 1969: VIII).
Because the *Untersuchungen* is concerned with the "Methodenstreit," it
is not really relevant to this study. It is, however, important to point out
several things. First, while Menger is concerned with economic theory,
he is also concerned with society and social phenomena (Menger 1969:
60–61, 79–80). Second, he is not promoting an abstract theory but is concerned with empirical reality. That means the real price of goods, the
real basic rents, and the real capital interest (Menger 1969: 69, 103–105).
Third, he takes issue with the claim of economic "'infallibility' and
'omniscience'" ("'Unfehlbarkeit' und 'Allweisheit'") (Menger 1969: 74).
Finally, Menger was not intending to discredit all German historians,
but he was ready to note that much of the German Historical School
was founded on Hegelian principles; principles which lend themselves
to claims of certainty and predictability (Menger 1969: 209, 221–222,
227–228). Rather than taking history as a partial basis from which to
develop an economic theory, the German Historical School chose to
build a political economy upon a philosophy of history.

While Menger is best known for his involvement in the
"Methodenstreit" and for his writings on subjective value, his major
focus was on money. This is shown by the numerous articles that he
published on money—its origins, its history, its value, and even its
future. As an indication of his appreciation for the importance of
money, Menger devoted the final chapter of his first book to an examination of it. Unfortunately, most scholars writing about Menger
do not have much regard for his theory of money with one major

exception: Erich W. Streissler. Streissler began his "Menger's Theories of Money and Uncertainty—A Modern Interpretation" with a story about a horse trader who sought to educate his son on economics. Streissler wrote "'My son, everything that is scarce is expensive. A good horse, for instance, is very scarce, so it is very expensive.' 'But, Dad,' asked the son, 'how come? Isn't a good horse that is cheap even scarcer?'" Streissler then notes that it is not the father but the son who has "the more interesting economic theory; and that it is this theory that is at the heart of Menger's analysis."[11] While this is an important point, it is secondary to the purpose here, which is to provide an account of Menger's ideas regarding money and to show how they more or less indicate a theory of money.

Menger on Money

Money in the Grundsätze

Menger concluded his *Grundsätze der* Volkswirthschaftslehre with the chapter on money. It has four sections, three of which are of considerable importance because they are focused on the essence and origins of money, its use, and its function as the measure of price. The fourth section is on metal coins. The chapter seems similar to many of the previous ones in that the title "Die Lehre vom Gelde" shares "Lehre" with many of the previous ones. However, "Die Lehre vom Gelde" differs from the earlier chapters in terms of form and substance. In terms of the former, Menger had utilized footnotes rather sparingly throughout the book; however, in this chapter there are footnotes on twenty-five of the thirty-five pages. More importantly, there are a number of pages devoted almost entirely to a footnote with the text taking up only two lines. Finally, there are a few footnotes which are carried over several pages.[12] In terms of the latter, Menger combines historical research with theory. There are, however, some similarities: Menger attempts to disprove traditional theories and he builds continuity with the preceding chapters on exchange. "Ueber das Wesen und den Ursprung des Geldes" begins with Menger noting that the chances of a successful exchange are not, as is customarily thought, plentiful, but are actually rather rare. That is because several things have to align just right: there needs to be two people who have goods that the other needs and they need to meet each other at the appropriate time. Menger offers three scenarios that illustrate the remote chance of a successful exchange. First, if person A has a sword that he has no need for and person B has a plow that he does not need, then it is easy for person A to exchange his unneeded sword for a much-needed plow and for person B to give his unneeded plow for the sword that he does need. But second, in the case of a person who has a fishing net that he no longer needs and wishes to exchange it for some hemp, how likely is it that such a person will find someone who both has the hemp and wishes to exchange it for a fishing net? Third, in the case of a person who owns land and has a horse but wishes to trade that horse for some farming tools and some clothes, although there may be some people in need of a horse, how many of them will have the required farming implements much less clothes that will fit the landowner? Menger's conclusion is that this is rather unlikely (Menger 1968b: 250–251). The high degree of unlikeliness prompts humans to find some way of increasing the odds for a successful exchange. This is because people do not have the luxury of going without certain things. Menger insists that the direct meeting of needs is the final goal of all economic striving of humans ("Die directe Deckung des Bedarfes ist das Endziel aller wirthschaftlichen Bestrebungen der Menschen.") (Menger 1968b: 252). That means that humans needed to find some means that would yield exchanges that would satisfy each other's needs. That means will turn out to be monies ("Gelde"), and its "essence" ("Wesen") will turn out to be the vehicle of exchange. Before setting that out, Menger turns to discussing the other part of this first section, the "origin" ("Ursprung") of money."

During the Homeric era, copper was not just the easiest metal to work with but also the most versatile. However, it was not the most popular means of payment; for that, the Greeks tended to use livestock and in particular cows. In this sense, one can say that cows were the first forms of "money."[13] One of the theses that Menger traditionally attacks is the claim that the state was the originator of money. As he has shown, money was developed by individuals with the need to facilitate exchanges. As he maintains, "Money is not a state invention, not a product of a legislative act" ("Das Geld ist keine staatliche Erfindung, nicht das Product eines legislative Actes") (Menger 1968b: 259).

In the second section entitled "On each people and to each age is the specific money" ("Ueber das jedem Volke und jedem Zeitalter eigenthümliche Geld") Menger repeats his claim that money is not a product of agreement between economizing men nor a product of any legislative act. Instead, it developed differently in various cultures and at different times (Menger 1968b: 260–261). He again reminds us that in ancient times, cows were the means of exchange, as such, they were "natural money" ("natürliches Geld") in contrast to what he refers to as "economic monies" ("ökonomische Geldes"). This leads Menger to discuss the history of money and he notes how livestock was the "currency" of the ancient Greeks and others in antiquity. He also indicates that copper was the oldest metal and was being used to make plows, weapons, and tools. Copper was used alongside silver and gold to make drinking vessels and jewelry. At some point, people transitioned from using livestock as money to using coins, but Menger insists that it did not happen all at once. Rather, he emphasizes that it occurred at different times in different places so that it is impossible to assign a time and a place for the introduction of economic money (Menger 1968b: 262–266). He also takes issue with the narrative that only European areas were economically advanced. He argues that the European conquerors found the people in Mexico to have a highly advanced economic structure. He furthermore suggested that similar cases were found in other parts of the globe; while he does not explicitly condemn the Europeans for their imperialism, there is a trace of sadness and anger that Europeans believed that only they had the right culture, the right politics, and the right economics (Menger 1968b: 267–270).

The third section is devoted to the claim that money is the measure of price and he notes that this is a long-standing thesis. It appears to have originated with Aristotle and continues to the present day. But this belief in an "objective" basis for value is false; as Menger had argued throughout the *Grundsätze,* value is determined subjectively. He also notes that metal coins give the sense that value lies in them; accordingly, having first discussed the essence and origin of money, Menger concludes his work with a section on metal money (Menger 1968b: 278–279). Menger notes that there are certain problems with precious metals used in coins: 1) whether the metal is genuine, 2) the degree of purity, and 3) the actual weight of the coin. Regarding 1) and 2), very few non-experts can determine whether a coin is made from the actual precious metal identified and even fewer non-experts can determine the degree of purity of that coin. Regarding 3), very few people walk around with a scale in order to ascertain the exact weight of the coin. These problems lead Menger to his final point: just as difficulties increase with the number of people exchanging things, difficulties increase as the number of coins increase needed to purchase something. Menger stops his discussion of money at the use of coins—the introduction of non-metal money was designed in part to further facilitate economic transactions (Menger 1968b: 279–285). However, Menger goes on to discuss paper money in many later works on money.[14]

Money in the "Geld" Articles

Menger's article "Geld" is justifiably famous, yet it causes a number of difficulties. First, there is an English translation from 1892. The translator was an English woman better known for her Eastern orientation than her scholarly translations of economic classics. Her translation is problematic but even more so is the fact that she gives the author's name as Karl Menger. Menger's name was Carl; "Karl" was Carl's son who became an economics scholar in his own right. Then there is the problem of editions. The first one appeared in 1892, the second in 1900, and the third in 1909. There are vast differences between the editions in terms of substance and in form. The 1892 edition is in Fraktur, the old German script, whereas the 1900 and 1909 versions are in modern print. Even more problematic is the major difference between the three—the first edition is some 20 pages while the second had grown to 56 and the third edition had expanded to 116. The 1892 article has 8 sections plus the literature; the 1900 article has 11 plus literature, and the 1909 article has 14 plus literature. In light of all this, there are numerous changes among the three editions. But the fact that Menger's article "Geld" was only replaced by von Wieser's in the fourth edition of the *Handwörterbuch der Staatswissenschaften* is a testament to Menger's enduring contribution to the theory of money.

The 1892 version of "Geld" mostly follows the format of the final chapter on money in the *Grundsätze*. That is partially because Menger is again interested in determining the origin and function of money and partially because he is concerned with debunking the prevailing ideas of how money came about and the continuing belief in its objective essence. Menger begins by noting that the shift from the exchange of things for other things to the exchange of things for "small, useless appearing metal discs" ("kleine, an sich nutzlos erscheinende Metalscheiben") appeared to such educated people as Savigny as nothing less than being "fully secretive" ("Geheimvoll"). This is especially the case when one considers how previously people used other goods for exchange—including animals, tea, and salt (Menger 1892: 730–731). The problem is how to explain this, and Menger suggests that there has been a failure to do so from antiquity to the present day. There is no agreement as to whether money is an organic member of the economic world or whether it is an economic anomaly that has been artificially imposed by governments. The mysterious nature of money has continued to plague thinkers, and Menger is convinced that that is largely because of the lack of a compelling theory of money. In the "Geld" article, Menger intends to offer a cursory explanation into the particular function of money. The task is to explain how money functions in the transaction between two competing individuals; that is, how one person will accept metal coins (of nominal value) in exchange for an object (of actual worth). To accomplish this involves not only answering the question of the origin of money, but also answering the question of the nature of money and its place in the circle of general goods.[15]

Originally, two individuals exchanged things that they needed immediately. Thus, the exchange was limited not only in terms of time and space but also in terms of quantity and even quality. Menger places extraordinary emphasis on temporal and spatial limitations: the exchange can occur only when the two people need what each other has at that time and the exchange must occur at a specified place. Because these factors severely limited the prospects of successful exchanges, people set out to develop the means to expand the opportunities for exchanges. The means that they found was "money" ("Geld") in the form of coins (Menger 1892: 732–733). But Menger cautions that this invention did not appear overnight and everywhere; it began to be used gradually by different people and at varying times (Menger 1892: 734–735). Echoing his final chapter in *Grundsätze,* Menger insists that "Money has not been developed through law" ("Das Geld ist nicht durch Gesetz entstanden") and that its origins lie in society and not in the state. In fact, the state's recognition of the function of money came long after the use of coins had been accepted (Menger 1892: 736–737).

Menger points especially to the use that money plays in capitalism, both as a means of exchange ("Tauschmittel") and as a means of payment ("Zahlungsmittel"). That is, it is the best instrument for loans which are the actual functions of capital investment. Money functions as an intermediate in the "Money markets" ("Geldmarkte") (Menger 1892: 738). Money is used successfully as a means of exchange but it is even more successful where used as a means of payment. Thus, Menger's primary focus differs from most of his predecessors. While they were obsessed with uncovering the "essence" ("Wesen") of money, Menger is preoccupied with the function of money. (Menger 1892: 738).

The function of money is the focus of section IV and Menger begins by again taking issue with his predecessors but also with the German Historical School. For each of them, the primary concern was with the essence of "money" when it should have been on its function. After all, there is little value in determining what something *is*, but there is considerable value in ascertaining what something *does*. Menger returns to the discussion about moving goods and how it is one thing to attempt to move light weight objects. But it is clearly something else when one tries to exchange two heavy objects. Menger's point is that money serves as a replacement for the buyer. This not only relieves the buyer from arranging transport of his heavy object, but it also frees him up in terms of time and space.[16] It also means that the exchange of money for goods can be expedited which saves even more time and is more efficient. This seems to be what Menger means when he talks about capitalization in this brief section IV.

The more difficult and the more contentious the subject, the more space Menger devoted to it. That is why section V—"Das Geld als Maßstab des Tauschwertes der Güter" ("Money as the Measure of the Exchange Value of Goods")—is lengthier than the other sections. Menger begins by again criticizing most of his predecessors for not understanding the function of money. He complains that their teachings rest upon the acceptance that the "exchange value of money" ("Tauschwert des Geldes") was at first unknown to us and is revealed only with an examination. As a result, their conception of the exchange value is variable depending on the time, place, and size of the goods. Menger objects to this, suggesting that this estimation is about as stable as quicksilver, which is to say, not of much help (Menger 1892: 739). That is why Menger devotes so much attention to the notion that money is the measure of the exchange value of goods. It is also why he brings up the notion of price because most economists had been convinced that price was mostly stable and was not subject to much actual variation. Streissler is extremely helpful here in clarifying Menger's points. Streissler points out that Menger's early work related to stock exchanges, and there he observed the fluctuation in prices. Prices were determined by demand and so they fluctuated as the demand increased or decreased. But Streissler points out that prices vary even in the same locality and on a single day." He further points to Menger's recognition in the *Grundsätze* that Menger was conscious of how prices varied in markets. They change in different places, in different time, and with different people (Streissler 1973: 170). Streissler's overall point is that Menger believed that uncertainty dominated economics—while most economists sought stability and equilibrium. Streissler's lecture is filled with the words: "uncertainty," "change," "flux," "fickle," "unplanned," and "unpredictable" (Streissler 1973: 167, 168, 170, 172, 176, 184).

Part of the problem that Menger sees is that economists tend to focus on an individual case whereby they lose sight of the variations one finds in considering a multiplicity of cases. This is a matter of focusing on the realistic aspects of the problem instead of the more idealistic ones (Menger 1892: 741). He underscores his approach by insisting that "the most general experience teaches us" ("allgemeinste Erfahrung lehrt uns") that there is often a discrepancy between supply and demand and that reveals a difference in terms of price. Instead of the price of grain simply being x, he insists that it is x plus y, because y reflects the specific market (Menger 1892: 742–743). This observation about differences in price due to different markets was one of the major points that von Wieser had made about Menger in his "Karl Menger" (sic) (Wieser 1928b). It also underlies Menger's observation that many economists regard money as possessing an "external exchange value" ("äußere Tauschwert") that is somehow rather fixed. Economists like to employ it because it appears stable, but that just masks the massive fluctuations. It also attributes to economics a rational and essential basis for money rather than noticing that it tends to be irrational and arbitrary (Menger 1892: 745). He advocates moving away from thinking that one can predict with reliable certainty toward a more probabilistic approach. And he again counsels aiding abstract theory by adding concrete examples. In addition, he suggests that instead of hoping for definitive numbers, that we should be satisfied with averages (Menger 1892: 746–747). Menger concludes this lengthy section with another reminder about the volatility in markets and prices and, by extension, to money (Menger 1892: 549–750).

In section V1 Menger addresses the matter of money as the measurement of prices. He begins by tackling the contention that in an exchange, both parties believe that their goods have equal value. Once again, Menger looks at the history of this belief, which he again traces back to Aristotle. Although it may seem accurate in theory, once again Menger maintains that it rarely holds true in practice. As he has argued previously, there are many variables which affect the value of each person's goods, so that there cannot be a standard or equal value. Rather, it is a subjective matter, and Menger refers to an article by Eugen Böhm-Bawerk and a book by Friedrich von Wieser to bolster his viewpoint.[17] Menger concludes this section with the insistence that money cannot be regarded as a standard of measure for the worth of an object (Menger 1892: 751).

Section VII is another one of the lengthier sections and that is because Menger is focused on proving that one errs in considering money as an object that has an essence. Instead, he wants to show that one can gain a concept of money only by looking at its function, hence the section's title "Aus seinen Funktionen ergebender Begriff des Geldes." He first mentions that there are different types of money and he lists some of them: "livestock money" ("Veihgeld"), "iron money" ("Eisengeld"), "coin money" (Barrengeld"), "paper money" ("Papiergeld"), and "credit money" ("Kreditgeld"). However, in general speech, it is simply regarded as money and as the means of exchange. Menger reminds us that the question about money is not merely terminological, but rather it is an issue of how the term money developed conceptually ("Begriffsentwicklung des Geldes") (Menger 1892: 751–752). But Menger repeats that economists are convinced that money is a thing and this is expressed by the propositions "that money is a good" ("Der Satz, 'daß das Geld eine Ware sei'") and "Money is an exchange object" ("Das Geld ist eine Verkehrsobjekt"), and that it has its own character (Menger 1892: 752–754). However, Menger argues that unlike other goods, money does not have any intrinsic worth. It does not have a nature and properties like other goods; its value lies in its function. Menger sums up by saying that "Money is no bare *signifier* of value." ("Das Geld ist kein bloßes *Zeichen* des Wertes.") It is equally false to insist that money is a good which is equal to all other goods. Instead, money is used to take care of human needs so the important thing is to understand how money is used to satisfy needs and wants (Menger 1892: 754).

Section VIII, Menger's final section, is devoted to the need for money in the economy ("Der Bedarf der Volkswirtschaft an Geld"). His sources here are Adam Smith, David Ricardo, and John Stuart Mill; however, he noted that he disagreed with them regarding the speed of money in circulation ("Umlaufsgeschwindigkeit"). Menger asserted that the classical economic theorists tended to overestimate the importance of the speed of circulation. Instead, it is a matter of the amount of money that is in circulation that is crucial. Rather than building a theory upon some standard view of circulatory speed, he insists that one needs to look at the specific economy (Menger 1892: 754–755). Menger concludes the first edition version of "Geld" by suggesting that money is the means of exchange but that in more progressive economies, it is the means of payment used by such institutions as banks of various kinds ("Depositenbanken, Sparkassen, u.s.f.") (Menger 1892: 756).

The first edition of "Geld" is neither too lengthy nor too complex; however, Menger was not satisfied with it and he apparently welcomed the opportunity to revise and expand it when offered the opportunity eight years later. In the same vein, Menger would again revise and expand his article for the third edition of the *Handwörterbuch der Staatswissenschaften*. As indicated earlier, the second and the third variations of "Geld" fundamentally differ in size and in substance. The investigations here into the later versions will note the similarities but will focus primarily on the substantial changes that Menger made for the 1900 version and for the 1909 one.

The major focus has been on the 1892 edition of "Geld" and for two reasons. First, it was Menger's most carefully thought-out conception of money. Second, it was the one which was, and continues to be, the best-known version. Yet, the second and third editions also need to be addressed. The changes that Menger made for the second edition are rather substantial. They include the addition of new chapters; in fact, only chapters 1, 6, 8, and the literature section are carried over into the next edition. One of the most significant changes is Menger's incorporation of secondary sources. Most, but not all of these, were publications which appeared between 1892 and 1899. A second and related change is the significant increase in the number and the lengths of footnotes. Previously, Menger had kept them to a brief citation; now they are lengthy excursions. A third major change is the shift from the emphasis on function to other, more contemporary issues. It is not clear whether he no longer felt the need to challenge the notion of money as substance or whether he felt that the new challenges about metal currency and the role of the state were more important.[18]

The issue of metal money was becoming an even more pressing issue because of the increasing importance of capitalism. Menger noted that throughout history coins continued to be refined but, unfortunately, the problem of their weight remained (Menger 1900: 73–75). In addition, there was the matter of the price of gold and whether it can be determined and regulated through any sort of system. These issues led Menger to address the role of the state in the development of money. (This was five years before Georg Friedrich Knapp would publish his statist theory of money.) Menger and others had been promoting the concept that money was a legal matter and that states had not just the right but the duty to introduce and regulate currencies. However, Menger continued to insist that money is not instituted by the state but through society (Menger 1900: 77–79). In chapter 6, Menger maintained that money is an economic means and not a legal one. In modern society, money allowed one to buy consumable and durable goods. Moreover, it allowed for credit and especially for capital. Thus, it had been transformed from a means of exchange to a means of advancing capitalism (Menger 1900: 81). To help justify these claims, Menger appealed to Adam Smith, Stanley Jevons, Alfred Marshall, Leon Walras, as well as his brother Anton Menger (Menger 1900: 86–90, 95 and various footnotes).

Menger returns to his attack on the idea that money is a legal instrument in chapter 10. There, he objects to the notion that the state can forcibly control the circulation of money. He is willing to grant that money can be considered from a legal standpoint but insists that that does not imply that the state can and should be involved in regulating money in circulation. Rather than a legal matter, money is solely an economic issue (Menger 1900: 101–103). Menger concludes with some final observations about the importance of payments for goods, both for immediate and credit for long-term purchases and how payment is crucial to a smoother functioning economy. He assumes that the need for metal currencies will be lessened as the need for easier forms of payment increases in the future (Menger 1900: 105).

The changes that Menger made for the third edition are rather mixed. In terms of minor changes, the literature section has been reduced and the footnotes have been pared back. It also seems as if Menger has not added much in the way of new sources, and that is readily apparent in one of the most significant additions to the 1909 edition. There is a new chapter 2 with the unwieldly title "Der Streit der Wirtschaftstheoriker und der Juristen über die Natur des Geldes und dessen Eigenart im Kreise der übrigen Güter." This may be rendered "The Conflict of the Economic Theorists and the Jurists over the Nature of Money and its Particularity in the Circle of General Goods." (Menger 1909: 565). It is divided into two sections with the first carrying the title "Der Streit der Wirtschaftstheoretiker" ("The Conflict of the Economic Theoreticians"). Menger indicates that the particularity of money is what has drawn the attention of economic theorists and, in particular, the fact that money does not have immediate use but acquires use during the somewhat lengthy process of exchange. This prompts the economic theorist to regard money as an anomaly. In turn, this leads some to conclude that the only way in which money can be regulated is by the state. Rather than being an "arbitrary value," the state supposedly renders it a "fact value." And, this leads some to maintain that money is actually a type of "goods" (Menger 1909: 565). Menger insists that this dispute is not simply a matter of semantics; rather, it goes to the heart of what people think money is and how it functions (Menger 1909: 566). He suggests that the salesman and the speculator have slightly different ideas about money but they agree that its value lies in what it does and not in what it is— as a "good" does (Menger 1909: 566–567).

Menger turns his attention in the second section to the conflict between the economists and the jurists and this is reflected in its title "Die Unterscheidung Zwischen 'Geld' und 'Ware' in der Jurisprudence" ("The Difference between 'Money' and "Goods' in Jurisprudence") (Menger 1909: 567). Menger argues that money is different from goods because of what it does: it allows for the exchange of goods in general. As such, money is a purely economic instrument, which allows for the exchange of goods but also serves as payment for loans. Again, this is a purely economic matter. Menger concludes that "It is no legislative arbitrary-thing, but rather the consequence of the particularity of money in the circulation of the general objects of exchange" ("Es ist keine legislative Willkürlichkeit, sondern eine Folge der Eigenart des Geldes im Kreis der übrigen Verkehrsobjekte") (Menger 1909: 568). Given that Menger has spent decades refuting the notion that the state is involved in the production and regulation of money, it is not surprising that he has devoted a separate section to this issue. What is surprising is that he has ignored the powerful claim by Georg Friedrich Knapp that the state is the originator and stabilizer of money and that it is obligated in doing so in order to provide a rational foreign exchange rate. This is what Knapp had argued in his *Staatliche Theorie des Geldes*, which appeared in 1905. It would be published as a second edition in 1918 and a third edition in 1921.[19] Knapp would author a new entry of the chartist theory of money for the fourth edition of the *Handwörterbuch der Staatswissenschaften*. This entry followed the one on "Geld"—which was then written by Friedrich von Weiser and was the last thing von Wieser published.

Money in the Other Articles

Menger published a number of brief articles on money and most of these appeared between 1889 and 1893, with one appearing in 1889, three appearing in 1892, and one the following year. These, along with the 1909 version of "Geld" are reprinted in volume 4 of Menger's *Gesammelte Schriften* with the title *Schriften über Geldtheorie and Währungspolitik (Writings on the Theory of Money and Currency Politics)*. These are occasional pieces and are mostly of historical interest. However, they contain comments that reflect Menger's conception of money. They also reflect his concern with the political consequences of currency politics, which helps dispute the claims by Menger's critics that his thinking is too abstract and too removed from peoples' lives.

    The first is a brief newspaper article devoted to the purchasing power of the Austrian currency. In "Die Kaufkraft des Guldens österreischischer Währung" Menger discusses how the purchasing power of money had shifted since 1879 and that it continued to reflect what he regarded as an anomaly. The anomaly was that there is a difference between the value of the silver and its market value and that foreigners have exploited that fact to the detriment of Austrians. He offers a comparison between the Austrian Gulden to the American dollar, the French Franc, and to the German Taler. His conclusion is that the Austrian Gulden has less buying power when compared with these other currencies and that Austrians suffer when buying foreign goods. In addition, the continuous fluctuation of the Gulden's value makes it more difficult for Austrians to plan for the future. In light of these problems, Menger insists that it is time that the government takes steps to address these problems (Menger 1970i: 119, 121–122).

The themes about the problems facing Austrians because of their currency and those ramifications will be carried into his writings from 1892 and 1893.

These themes are also revealed in his February 1892 newspaper article "On our Currency Exchange" ("Von unserer Valuta"). There, Menger argued that the Austrian currency was one of the most remarkable anomalies in the history of money and that is because its exchange value is divorced from its "inner value." Menger contrasts the Austrian currency with the German Mark and the French Francs and how both of those have an "inner value" that is reflected in its exchange value (Menger 1970j: 287). He argued that the disparity in exchange values hurts Austria's economy because the value of silver continues to drop. Menger is promoting that gold be used, but he clarifies that he does not belittle bi-metalism. (Menger 1970j: 296, 299). But his concern is with how the problems with the Austrian currency affect not only the big people with their big money but also the "little man" ("Kleiner Mann") with their "little possessions" ("kleine Besitze") (Menger 1970j: 306–307).

Menger continued with his recommendation that Austria changes from silver to gold currency in a pamphlet published in the summer of 1892. That which indicates his recommendation is the subtitle connecting the pamphlet with Menger's February newspaper article: *Der Übergang zur Goldwährung. Untersuchungen über die Wertprobleme der Österreichisch-Ungarischen Valutareform.* In the "Vorwort" he explicitly recalls the anomaly that plagued the Austrian silver currency. Menger provides numerous statistics in support of his thesis, and economic historians may be inclined to debate them. But Menger's objective is to help determine currency policy and that is why much of his discussion appears directed toward the government (Menger 1970k: 201, 207, 210). The overriding concern in his pamphlet is the stability of the currency's value and the defense of Austria's monetary reform (Menger 1970k: 213).

Menger continued his positive assessment of the transition to gold in an essay "Das Goldagio und der heutigen Stand der Valutareform" which appeared in June 1893 and then as a separate pamphlet. He argued that the initial assessment of these monetary reforms were both necessary and beneficial (Menger 1970l: 308–310). While he warned of an immediate turbulent future, he assured his readers that these monetary reforms will prove to have lasting benefits for the money markets and for the banks (Menger 1970l: 324). While his comments do not have much bearing on his theory of money, they again undermine the critics' claims that his thinking is too abstract and divorced from reality.

Concluding Comments

This chapter had two goals. The first was to offer an account of Menger's general economic thought, ranging from his early methodological works to his later more specific articles. To achieve that goal entailed a discussion of his methodological writings and emphasizing how he combined theory with examples. The aim was to counter the criticism that Menger's theories were too abstract and far removed from reality. It showed instead that Menger was keenly aware of the need to explain economics in social terms. The second goal was to investigate Menger's writings on money. This meant beginning with the final chapter in his *Grundsätze* and then devoting most of that section to the various editions of his *Handwörterbuch der Staatswissenschaften* article on "Geld," and culminating with some of his occasional writings on money. While Menger's reputation largely rests on his involvement in the "Methodenstreit," this chapter reveals a far nuanced and a more receptive thinker—and an expert on method and on money.[20]

Notes

1 "Als Babeuf vor der Guillotine stand, bekümmerte ihn, der den Tod nicht fürchtete, nur der Gedanke, dass die Geschichte seiner Bestrebungen von seinen Gegern geschrieben werden könnte." Menger 1970d: 220. An indication of this is found in the article "Schmoller" in *Palgrave's Dictionary of Political Economy*. There Menger is accused of seriously misjudging Gustav Schmoller and his friends and is criticized as misrepresenting Schmoller's true views. The various editions of the *Palgrave* usually contain well written and objective accounts of the people and ideas, but the one on Schmoller is a real departure. It was written by Broadus Mitchell who was at the time a professor of economics at Johns Hopkins but was forced to leave in the early 1930s because of his radical views. In "Schmoller" Mitchell paints a portrait of Schmoller as a most enlightened scholar and man of principles, yet most accounts by numerous people have revealed that he bordered on abusing his power as educator and even more as editor. Mitchell 1926: 753.
2 Carl Menger's son, Karl Menger, addressed some of these complaints in a paper he delivered at the 1971 conference held in honor of the

centennial of the publication of his father's *Grundsätze.* Karl Menger noted that as Menger's son and as a mathematician, he has "two souls," thus he is entitled to address the claim that Carl Menger was too concerned with mathematical formulations. Karl argued that the Early Austrians in general and his father in particular did not use mathematics but formulated their views verbally. Karl Menger 1973: 38–39. Erich Streissler countered the claim that Menger was uninterested in practical concerns by pointing out that he was the Austrian Crown Prince's personal tutor and that he became interested in economics largely because of his newspaper investigations into the Viennese stock market. Streissler 1973: 165. In his "Karl Menger" (sic), Friedrich von Wieser not only wrote a moving tribute of his master but explained how Menger influenced Böhm-Bawerk and him. Von Wieser also explained that Menger was drawn to study economics because of his observations of the Viennese markets. Von Wieser 1929: 117. Von Wieser's article "Menger, Carl" in *Palgrave's Dictionary of Political Economy* is also recommended reading on Menger. Von Wieser defends Menger from the charge that his theory of value was taken over from Gossen without acknowledgement on the grounds that Gossen's book had been rejected and that Menger had developed his theory independently. Von Wieser does suggest that Menger did not pursue his theory of value but turned to methodological issues. As a result, it was von Wieser and Böhm-Bawerk who continued Menger's work and should be regarded as founders of the Austrian School. Von Wieser does mention Menger's "Geld" article. Von Wieser 1926b: 924. Finally, in his article "The Austrian School of Economists" von Wieser insisted that Menger founded a new school in that he founded it on subjective value and that he was concerned with facts. Von Wieser 1926a: 814–815.

3 Given how much Menger wrote on money, it is remarkable that so little has been written about it. Even Erich Streissler, who is one of the greatest authorities on Menger has little to say about it. The paper that he presented at the 1971 conference is ostensibly devoted to it—"Menger's Theories of Money and Uncertainty—A Modern Interpretation"—has little to do with Menger's articles on "Geld." Streissler cites the *Grundsätze* eight times whereas he cited "Geld" only three times. Furthermore, he lists the first edition as appearing in 1891 when it appeared a year later and he suggests that the third edition was basically unchanged from the second. As will be shown, that is incorrect. Streissler 1973: 165–166 and note 1. In von Wieser's "Karl Menger" (sic), "Geld" is not even mentioned either as Menger's article or even as a concept. Von Wieser 1929.

4 F.A. Hayek reminded us that when Menger's *Grundsätze* was first published, "it was only ninety-five years since the *Wealth of Nations,* only fifty-four years since Ricardo's *Principles,* and a mere twenty-three years since the great restatement of classical economics by John Stuart Mill." Hayek also pointed out that Menger's early work had a limited readership and that it was through the works by Böhm-Bawerk and von Wieser that Menger's theories finally attracted some real attention. Hayek 1973: 1, 11.

5 "On the Essence of Goods" ("Ueber das Wesen der Güter"), "On the Essence and Origin of the Value of Goods" ("Ueber das Wesen und Ursprung des Güterwerthes"), and "On the Essence and Origin of Money" ("Ueber das Wesen und Ursprung des Gelds").

6 Because Menger's conclusion in his "Vorrede" is so conciliatory, it is worth quoting in full: "Möge diese Schrift desshalb auch als ein freundlicher Gruss eines Mitstrebenden aus Oesterreich betrachtet werden, als ein schwacher Widerhall der wissensschaftlichen Anregungen, welche uns Oesterreichern von Deutschland aus durch so viele ausgezeichnete Gelehrte, die es uns sandte, und durch seine vortrefflichen Schriften in so reichlichem Masse zu Theil geworden sind." Menger 1968a: III, X. It is beyond the scope of this book to document how much Menger wanted approval from the members of the German Historical School and how poorly they responded to him. Schmoller was particularly rude to Menger.

7 In 1889, Menger had praised Friedrich List as being the greatest German national economist and he regarded List's *Nationales System der politischen Oekonomie* (1841) as a path-breaking work. Menger also extolled List's practical achievements, including his argument for the need for national duties and his support for the infant German railways. Menger 1970e: 247, 252–253, 256. Another indication of Menger's respect for some of the leaders of the German Historical School is found in his lengthy review of the second edition of Gustav Schönberg's *Handbuch der politischen Oekonomie.* Menger insists that the work addresses a pressing need, is composed of clear and insightful essays written by well-respected specialists, and should be warmly welcomed from every friend of political economy no matter where he is located. Menger 1970f: 101–102. Menger singles out the German scholars Wilhelm Lexis, Johannes Conrad, and Schönberg himself for praise. Menger's criticisms will be discussed below.

8 "Vermögen." Menger notes that the term is difficult to define and that has to do not just with the idea of ownership but also the notion of "availability" ("Verfügbar"). Menger 1968b: 70 and notes * and **.

9 Menger 1968b: 85–86. It is not known how much philosophy Menger knew, but Menger's subjective theory of value is similar to Kant's epistemology. Until Kant, philosophers tended to believe that knowledge copied reality and so knowledge was accurate if it was objective. Kant's "Copernican" turn showed that rather than objects making knowledge possible, there were epistemological preconditions which even made knowledge of objects possible. These were time and space, but also causality. These did not belong to objects themselves, but were found in the subject's mind. That they were subjective did not make them relative; in fact, their universality and necessity guaranteed their validity. Menger's point is that demonstrating that value is not inherent in the thing but is a recognition that it is valuable to me, does not render it less valuable.

10 The other work that Menger wrote in connection to the "Methodenstreit" is an even different kind of work. "Die Irrtümer des Historismus in der deutschen Nationalökonomie" (1884) is not a conventional essay by any means. Instead, it is a collection of seventeen "letters" that Menger had addressed to a friend. While it appears to be aimed at reforming German economic thought, its substance and its tone belie that. Because his work had been ignored or dismissed by Schmoller and others, Menger had come to the realization that there could be no genuine reform of the German Historical School. It was clear that Menger had come to regard Schmoller as an enemy—just that he had arrived at that position later

than Schmoller, who had long regarded Menger as a danger. Menger 1970g: 1–3, 39–40, 67–70, 96–97. Menger was incensed that Schmoller accused him of complaining about Roscher and Hildebrand's economic writings, when he did no such thing. He complained that Schmoller accused him of being an adherent to "Manchesterism" when he was not. And, he complained that Schmoller accused him of being sympathetic to mysticism, when he was an economic theorist. Menger 1970g: 80.

11 Streissler 1973: 164. Streissler is one of most helpful commentators on Menger who I have read. That is why his remark that Menger's "Geld" is found in the "1ˢᵗ to 3ʳᵈ edn." of the *Handwörterbuch der Staatswissenschaften* is troubling. Streissler 1973: 166, note 1. A comparison of the three editions shows a substantial difference between the first and second and rather minimal changes between the second and third. Perhaps the answer is that he was quoting from the third edition that was contained in *The Collected Works of Carl Menger* from 1936.

12 For one example, the footnote * which begins on page 255, ends on page 260! For another example, the footnote * which begins on page 261 ends on the next page. For a third example, the footnote * which begins on page 276 ends on the next page. For a fourth example, the footnote * which begins on page 278 ends on the next page. For a fifth example, the footnote * which begins on page 282 ends on the next page. On page 263, there are five footnotes.

13 In footnote * to page 254, Menger provides a lengthy account of the term for money in many different languages. In the huge footnote * to pages 255 to 260, he discusses how advanced cultures used silver and gold for exchange.

14 Earlier in this chapter Menger suggested that there came a point at which "natural money" was replaced by "economic money" and that is finally being replaced by money in general. Menger 1968b: 264. Menger 1970 b, h.

15 "eine Frage nicht nur des Ursprungs, sondern auch des Wesens des Geldes und seiner Stellung im Kreise der übringen Güter." Menger 1892: 731–732.

16 It is worth noting that the sole German scholar who Menger singles out for some praise was Karl Knies and he does so several times. Menger cites the 1873 edition of *Geld und Kredit* once and the second edition of 1885 three times. Menger 1892: 734 note 1; 735 note 1, 738 note 1, 739 note 1. It needs to be said that Knies first published *Geld und Kredit* in separate volumes and when he revised it in 1885, he only revised *Geld*. It is also worth noting that *Geld* is not entirely a work on money. The first part is on capital and the second is on use. The third part is devoted to money. Even though the part on money is the longest, it is also a critique of Marxism and a defense of the legal foundation of money. See Knies 1873: 105–143 and 223–257. As with Carl Menger, this work was published with the name Carl Knies. It may also be worth noting that in "Geld," Menger cites Böhm-Bawerk and Friedrich von Wieser with approval. Menger 1892: 751 note 2.

17 Böhm-Bawerk's article was "Grundzüge der Theorie des wirtschafltichen Güterwertes" and von Wieser's book was *Der natürliche Werth*. Menger also mentions a book by Emil Sax and a book by R. Zuckerkandl. He also refers to his own *Grundsätze*. Menger 1892: 751 note 2.

18 These were all changes that Menger made but there is one signif-
    icant change between the 1892 edition of the *Handwörterbuch der
    Staatswissenschaften* and the 1900 edition that the editors and/or the pub-
    lishers made. That was the decision to switch from Fraktur to the more
    typical font. It is not clear what prompted this change because at the time,
    most Germans could read Fraktur, but that has not been the case for
    many decades. Although much of the Nazi propaganda from the 1920s
    and 1930s were printed in Fraktur, the Nazis wanted their information to
    reach the world, so in January of 1941, they formally banned it and imme-
    diately stopped it being taught in school. With the exception of some
    scholars, very few people are able to read it. In my experience Germans
    are reluctant to admit they lack the ability. I once loaned a friend the
    1921 edition of Max Weber's *Gesammelte Politischen Schriften* which was
    printed in Fraktur and the friend sheepishly returned it three weeks later
    with the admission that he could not read it. For several years I taught at
    Zeppelin Universität in Friedrichshafen. Zeppelin is a private, interna-
    tional school and is extremely expensive compared to German universi-
    ties and it draws students from wealthy backgrounds. At the beginning
    of my first semester teaching there I brought in an old copy of Ferdinand
    Tönnies' *Gemeinschaft und Gesellschaft*. This was the first meeting of the
    course and I passed it around with everyone indicating that they could
    read it. Much later, a number of students privately admitted that they
    could not read it but thought that they should claim to do so. The local
    paper in Traunstein where I live, shifted the Saturday insert from Fraktur
    to regular font; only keeping the title to the insert in Fraktur. And, that
    was around 2010. I have received confirmation from scholars who have
    lived and studied in Germany and who are specialists on early twentieth
    century German thinkers that outside of a handful of them, not many for-
    eigners can read it. I have also gotten confirmation from German schol-
    ars that it is an ability that not too many people now have.
19 Knapp's theory drew considerable attention and one of the most notable
    authors was Max Weber. In the first part of *Wirtschaft und Gesellschaft*,
    he devoted an entire appendix ("Exkurs") to Knapp's theory. Weber
    1922: 109–113.
20 It is important to keep in mind that Menger was regarded as one
    of the leading authorities on money for decades. The fact that he
    authored the article "Geld" for three editions of the *Handwörterbuch
    der Staatswissenschaften* is a testament to his expertise. One wonders
    whether he would have authored the fourth edition had he been alive
    or whether Knapp's statist theory of money had rendered Menger's
    anti-legal approach temporarily obsolete. It is interesting that it was von
    Wieser who wrote the article "Geld" for the fourth edition. That article
    will be briefly discussed in the next chapter.

References

Borch, K. (1973) "The Place of Uncertainty in the Theories of the Austrian
    School." In Hicks J.R. and Weber W. (eds.), *Carl Menger and the Austrian
    School of Economics*. Oxford: At the Clarendon Press. 61–74.

Caldwell, B.J. (ed.) (1990) *Carl Menger and His Legacy in Economics*. Annual Supplement to Volume 22, History of Political Economy. Durham and London: Duke University Press.

Hayek, F.A. (1973) "The Place of Menger's Grundsätze in the History of Economic Thought. In Hicks J.R. and Weber W. (eds.), *Carl Menger and the Austrian School of Economics*. Oxford: At the Clarendon Press. 1–14.

Hutchison, T.W. (1973) "Some Themes from Investigations into Method." In Hicks J.R. and Weber W. (eds.), *Carl Menger and the Austrian School of Economics*. Oxford: At the Clarendon Press. 15–37.

Knies, C. (1873) *Geld und Kredit/Das Geld. Darlegung der Grundlehren von dem Gelde, mit einer Verörterung über das Kapital und die Uebertragung der Nutzungen*. Berlin: Weidmannische Buchhandlung.

Menger, C. (1892) "Geld." In *Handwörterbuch der Staatswissenschaften*. Herausgegeben von J. Conrad, L. Elster, W. Lexis, Edg. Loening. Jena: Verlag von Gustav Fischer. Dritter Band. Edelmetalte-Gewerkschaft. 730–757.

Menger, C. (1900) "Geld." In *Handwörterbuch der Staatswissenschaften*. Herausgegeben von J. Conrad, L. Elster, W. Lexis, Edg. Loening. Jena: Verlag von Gustav Fischer. Zweite, gänzlich umgearbeitete Auflage. Vierter Band. Galiani-v. Justi. 60–106.

Menger, C. (1909) "Geld." In *Handwörterbuch der Staatswissenschaften*. Herausgegeben von J. Conrad, L. Elster, W. Lexis, Edg. Loening. Jena: Verlag von Gustav Fischer. Dritte, gänzlich umgearbeitete Auflage. Vierte Band. 1–116.

Menger, C. (1968a)[1935] *Gesammelte Schriften*. Herausgegeben mit einer Einleitung und einem Schriftenverzeichnes von F.A. Hayek. Tübingen: J.C.B. Mohr (Paul Siebeck). 2. Auflage. Band I.

Menger, C. (1968b) "Grundsätze der Volkswirthschaftslehre. Erster, Allgemeiner Theil." In *Gesammelte Schriften*. Herausgegeben mit einer Einleitung und einem Schriftenverzeichnes von F.A. Hayek. Tübingen: J.C.B. Mohr (Paul Siebeck). 2. Auflage. Band I. X–285.

Menger, C. (1969) "Untersuchungen über die Methode der Sozialwissenschaften und der politischen Ökonomie Inbesondere." In *Gesammelte Schriften*. Herausgegeben mit einer Einleitung und einem Schriftenverzeichnes von F.A. Hayek. Tübingen: J.C.B. Mohr (Paul Siebeck). 2. Auflage. Band II.

Menger, C. (1970a) "Wilhelm Roscher." In *Gesammelte Schriften*. Herausgegeben mit einer Einleitung und einem Schriftenverzeichnes von F.A. Hayek. Tübingen: J.C.B. Mohr (Paul Siebeck). 2. Auflage. Band III. Kleinere Schriften zur Methode und Geschichte der Volkswirtschaftslehre. 273–282.

Menger, C. (1970b) "Zur Theorie des Kapitals." In *Gesammelte Schriften*. Herausgegeben mit einer Einleitung und einem Schriftenverzeichnes von F.A. Hayek. Tübingen: J.C.B. Mohr (Paul Siebeck). 2. Auflage. Band III. Kleinere Schriften zur Methode und Geschichte der Volkswirtschaftslehre. 135–183.

Menger, C. (1970c) "Grundzüge einer Klassifikation der Wirtschaftswissenschaften." In *Gesammelte Schriften*. Herausgegeben mit einer Einleitung und einem Schriftenverzeichnes von F.A. Hayek. Tübingen: J.C.B. Mohr (Paul Siebeck). 2. Auflage. Band III. Kleinere Schriften zur Methode und Geschichte der Volkswirtschaftslehre. 185–218.

Menger, C. (1970d) "Die Social-Theorien der classischen National-Oekonomie und die moderne Wirtschaftspolitik." In *Gesammelte Schriften*. Herausgegeben mit einer Einleitung und einem Schriftenverzeichnes von F.A. Hayek. Tübingen: J.C.B. Mohr (Paul Siebeck). 2. Auflage. Band III. Kleinere Schriften zur Methode und Geschichte der Volkswirtschaftslehre. 219–245.

Menger, C. (1970e) "Friedrich List." In *Gesammelte Schriften*. Herausgegeben mit einer Einleitung und einem Schriftenverzeichnes von F.A. Hayek. Tübingen: J.C.B. Mohr (Paul Siebeck). 2. Auflage. Band III. Kleinere Schriften zur Methode und Geschichte der Volkswirtschaftslehre. 247–257.

Menger, C. (1970f) "Kritik der Politischen Oekonomie." In *Gesammelte Schriften*. Herausgegeben mit einer Einleitung und einem Schriftenverzeichnes von F.A. Hayek. Tübingen: J.C.B. Mohr (Paul Siebeck). 2. Auflage. Band III. Kleinere Schriften zur Methode und Geschichte der Volkswirtschaftslehre. 99–131.

Menger, C. (1970g) "Die Irrtümer des Historismus in der deutschen Nationalökonomie." In *Gesammelte Schriften*. Herausgegeben mit einer Einleitung und einem Schriftenverzeichnes von F.A. Hayek. Tübingen: J.C.B. Mohr (Paul Siebeck). 2. Auflage. Band III. Kleinere Schriften zur Methode und Geschichte der Volkswirtschaftslehre. 3–98.

Menger, C. (1970h) "Beiträge zur Währungsfrage in Oesterreich-Ungarn." In *Gesammelte Schriften*. Herausgegeben mit einer Einleitung und einem Schriftenverzeichnes von F.A. Hayek. Tübingen: J.C.B. Mohr (Paul Siebeck). 2. Auflage. Band IV. Schriften über Geld und Währungspolitik. 125–187.

Menger, C. (1970i) "Die Kraftkraft des Guldens österreichischer Währung." In *Gesammelte Schriften*. Herausgegeben mit einer Einleitung und einem Schriftenverzeichnes von F.A. Hayek. Tübingen: J.C.B. Mohr (Paul Siebeck). 2. Auflage. Band IV. Schriften über Geld und Währungspolitik. 117–125.

Menger, (1970j) "Von unserer Valuta." In *Gesammelte Schriften*. Herausgegeben mit einer Einleitung und einem Schriftenverzeichnes von F.A. Hayek. Tübingen: J.C.B. Mohr (Paul Siebeck). 2. Auflage. Band IV. Schriften über Geld und Währungspolitik. 287–307.

Menger, C. (1970k) "Der Übergang zur Goldwährung. Untersuchungen über die Wirtprobleme der Österreichisch-Ungarischen Valutareform." In *Gesammelte Schriften*. Herausgegeben mit einer Einleitung und einem Schriftenverzeichnes von F.A. Hayek. Tübingen: J.C.B. Mohr (Paul Siebeck). 2. Auflage. Band III. Kleinere Schriften zur Methode und Geschichte der Volkswirtschaftslehre. 189–224.

Menger, C. (1970l) "Das Goldagio und der heutige Stand der Valutareform." In *Gesammelte Schriften*. Herausgegeben mit einer Einleitung und einem Schriftenverzeichnes von F.A. Hayek. Tübingen: J.C.B. Mohr (Paul Siebeck). 2. Auflage. Band IV. Schriften über Geld und Währungspolitik. 308–324.

Menger, K. (1973) "Austrian Marginalism and Mathematical Economics." In Hicks J.R. and Weber W. (eds.), *Carl Menger and the Austrian School of Economics*. Oxford: At the Clarendon Press. 38–60.

Mitchell, Broadus (1926) "Schmoller, Gustav." In Higgens H. (ed.), *Palgrave's Dictionary of Political Economy*. Vol. III. N–Z. London: Macmillan and Co. 751–753.

Streissler, E. (1973) "Menger's Theory of Money and Uncertainty—a Modern Interpretation." In Hicks J.R. and Weber W. (eds.), *Carl Menger and the Austrian School of Economics*. Oxford: At the Clarendon Press. 164–189.

Weber, M. (1922) *Grundriss der Sozialökonomik. III. Abteilung Wirtschaft und Gesellschaft*. Tübingen: Verlag von J.C.B. Mohr (Paul Siebeck).

Wieser, F. von (1926a) "The Austrian School of Economists." In Higgens H. (ed.), *Palgrave's Dictionary of Political Economy*. Vol. I. A–E. London: Macmillan and Co. 814–818.

Wieser, F. von (1926b) "Menger, Carl." In Higgens H. (ed.), *Palgrave's Dictionary of Political Economy*. Vol. II. F–M. London: Macmillan and Co. 923–924.

Wieser, F. von (1929) "Karl Menger." In *Gesammelte Abhandlungen*. Mit einer biographischen Einleitung. Herausgegeben von Friedrich A. v. Hayek. Tübingen: Verlag von J.C.B. Mohr (Paul Siebeck). 110–125.

3 Von Wieser and Value

Friedrich von Wieser

Von Wieser

One of the biggest criticisms of the Early Austrian School members was that they held "the doctrine of value as the cardinal point in economic theory" (Bonar 1926: 73). This was true of Menger and Böhm-Bawerk, but it was even truer of Friedrich von Wieser because much of his scholarly writings were devoted to the concept of value.[1] That is why some critics focused their attacks on von Wieser. One of the most important of these opponents was James Bonar.

James Bonar, an economist and a former Master of the Mint in Canada, wrote a brief entry on the "Austrian School of Economists" for the 1926 edition of the *Palgrave's Dictionary of Political Economy*. Besides being very short, it was neither very informative nor completely correct. Bonar seemed to side with the German Historical School as evidenced by his assertion that it was being "threatened in Austria (if not in Germany) by a group of writers who have returned to the deductive method" (Bonar 1926: 73). The fact that he referred to them as "writers" was likely intended to diminish their standing; insisting they were "threatening" probably served to undermine their legitimacy. Bonar's claim that they "returned to the deductive method" was most likely designed to show that they were Manchesterites in spirit and that they were seriously mistaken in substance.[2] Bonar's attempt to discredit the Austrian School did not seem to succeed. That Bonar's account of the Austrian School of Economists was faulty is supported by the fact that the editor of the Palgrave assigned von Wieser to write an additional article for *Palgrave's Dictionary*. Von Wieser's article carries the same title ("Austrian School of Economists") and, at four pages in length, is more comprehensive than Bonar's piece. Von Wieser's article is worth examining in some detail for three reasons: 1) it provides a corrective to Bonar's article; 2) it is written by one of the

DOI: 10.4324/9781003193746-3

three early Austrian economists; and 3) as it is a later work, it provides a powerful context for examining not only the Austrian School but also von Wieser's entire thinking. Finally, von Wieser's article spells out many of the differences that he had in regard to his mentor Menger.

Von Wieser began by noting that Carl Menger founded the Austrian School with the 1871 publication of his *Grundsätze* but he offers several points worth mentioning in some detail. First, he claimed that Menger was following the German Historical School in its rejection of the classical economists. Where he departed from the German Historical members was his unwillingness to repudiate all theory. In fact, he strove to introduce a more exact theory based upon the notion of subjective value. Von Wieser admits that Menger was not alone in this: Stanley Jevons and Léon Walras had so much as the same idea and that something similar was to be found in Gossen too. However, von Wieser insisted that all four differed in particulars and that Menger was the farthest away from the classical theorists. In fact, von Wieser maintained that the system that Menger and his followers had devised was not merely some modification of the classical system but was a completely new theory. Von Wieser pointed to the main difference: the classical economists were individualists. However, the classical economists were uninterested in the idea of subjective value. It was Menger's great contribution to show that value in exchange is dependent on the subjective value and that economics cannot be understood without it. Von Wieser wrote "It is Menger's great merit that he went back to the individual roots of economic facts" (von Wieser 1926: 814). But von Wieser maintained that his successors were determined to go beyond Menger's individualism and he added that "Wieser, especially, teaches that in national economy individuals are subject to social forces" (von Wieser 1926: 815). Von Wieser argues that the Austrians differ from the classical economists regarding the importance of the notion of freedom.[3] For the earlier thinkers, freedom was their "postulate." But for the Austrians, the economy required protections and that meant some limitations on freedom. It also implied that economists needed to consider the state in connection to the national economy and the national economy in relation to the world's economy (von Wieser 1926: 815).

According to von Wieser, Menger distinguished between free goods and economic goods. Free goods are those in abundance so there is no economic value in them. In other words, with free goods, supply is greater than demand; but with economic goods, demand is greater than the supply. Von Wieser adds that with free goods, there is no need for forethought but with economic goods one needs to consider the future. Value then, is what we attribute to a thing for its ability to satisfy our need. One can construct a line from that object which can least fill our need to that object that can most fully satisfy our want. Von Wieser does not mention that Menger did not give a name to that which fully satisfies our need, but he does mention that he had given this the term "marginal utility" ("Grenznutzen"), and Jevons referred to it as "the final degree of utility." Von Wieser defines marginal utility as being "based on the law of satisfaction of want, which states that the degree of desire for the same amount of goods diminishes with continuous satiation" (von Wieser 1926: 815). Menger and the Austrians joined Gossen, Walras, and Jevons in believing that this law was all important. For details, he directs the reader to the article "Final Degree of Utility" in the second volume of *Palgrave's Dictionary of Political Economy*.[4]

Von Wieser makes the observation that marginal utility does not just apply to economic goods, but also to economic systems once they have reached a particular degree of sophistication and then it also applies to labor. He clarifies that in primitive cultures labor is free because it is based upon slaves. But in advanced industrialized economies, labor has become specialized. Von Wieser points out that even Adam Smith admitted slave labor was not totally free because of the workers' requirements of "rest, freedom, and happiness" (von Wieser 1926: 815). But he adds that Smith's theory is fundamentally a theory of labor, but one which he did not fully work out. It was left to Ricardo to do so, and then his theory was accepted by the socialists. Von Wieser's point is that in modern economies, this theory does not hold because if there is insufficient labor then it becomes similar to any economic good in respect to the law of marginal utility. Von Wieser granted that the law of marginal utility is not easy to understand and it is often obscured in practice. Rather than looking to Menger to help explain it, von Wieser turned to Böhm-Bawerk. According to Böhm-Bawerk, the lowest order, or the proximate order, are those objects that are needed immediately to satisfy a need. For a hungry person, that would be a loaf of bread. The second order is that which helps make the bread; in this case, it is the flour. Von Wieser suggested that this continues until one reaches the highest order; that is, that which cannot be produced. One example of the higher order is the land— because it cannot be produced. Another example is labor; while it produces things, labor itself cannot be produced. Von Wieser explained that the value is derived from the first order goods. Menger held that the value of the higher order could not be determined because there were too many parts; von Wieser and Böhm-Bawerk have offered a different approach. Von Wieser did not discuss what his brother-in-law

Böhm-Bawerk had proposed, but he did explain his own method. He referred to this as "practical imputation" ("Zurechnung") and he compared this to an approach used in law. Just as the law punishes the "responsible originator," the economist wants to determine the causes of production. He distinguished between specific and general imputation with the former applying to specific things like a mine, whereas the latter applies to the more widely distributed elements, which he identified as labor, coal, or iron. He clarified this by indicating that forest land has little value when there is plentiful wood, but a vineyard is valued if it produces a special vintage (von Wieser 1926: 815–816).

Von Wieser spent much of the remainder of this article discussing the differences between Menger and himself. For Menger, value was only subjective because it involved individuals, but for von Wieser, value was also objective because it was the value of the national economy. Another difference was about money: Menger was content to uncover the origin of money but von Wieser developed his theory based upon marginal utility. In addition, Menger remained a convinced metallist but he claimed that his position was between mentalism and nominalism. Thus, money does not just possess value because of its material but also because of its use in exchange. More than that, it is used in taxation and thus has an additional value (von Wieser 1926: 816). Menger not only neglected that topic, but he did not offer a theory of income. As a result, he provided only a few comments on capital and interest, and it was left to Böhm-Bawerk to give an exhaustive account. Von Wieser complimented Böhm-Bawerk for his masterful account of the history of capital but explained that he differed with him on the notion of income. He claimed that he wrote a complete account of the theory of income and he sketched a few points here.[5] Income is derived through prices which are subject to the law of marginal utility. The problem with Ricardo's account of agricultural rent is that although it is backed up empirically, it is lacking in a theoretical framework. Because Ricardo was unfamiliar with the law of marginal utility, he did not recognize that agricultural land possessed specific imputation. In contrast, urban rent possesses general imputation. The entrepreneur's income is highest because he is a single individual, whereas the laborer's wages are the lowest because he is a member of a very large class (von Wieser 1926: 817–818).

Von Wieser offered a few concluding comments, and most of them focused on the differences between himself and others. He insisted that Germans misunderstood Menger's subjective value because they erroneously regarded it to be psychological, whereas it was in fact simply economics. He also suggested that he and others have gone beyond

Menger because they considered economics in terms of states—hence, the objective side that Menger had mostly ignored. He closed with the observation that the Austrian School had gradually won adherents from all parts of the world; finally, even from Germany (von Wieser 1926: 817).

In 1890 von Wieser was invited by the editor of *The Economic Journal* to write an article explaining the basic tenets of the Austrian journal in its inaugural issue.[6] Von Wieser began "The Austrian School and the Theory of Value" by indicating the ideas that it shared. Despite their differences, the Austrian School and the German Historical School shared the rejection of speculation for the reliance on observation. Despite the terminological differences, which the Austrians share with the English, both schools look at the empirical evidence like a cartographer draws his map. Evidence is not meant to deceive but to represent; just as those who can read maps will better find their way, those who can understand economic theories will better understand how markets work and value is ascertained (von Wieser 1901: 108).

Von Wieser reminds his readers that that which is superabundant has little or no value; scarcity helps determine value. The problem with many previous economic thinkers was that they believed that labor was the sole determinant of value. However, von Wieser insisted that value is determined by the combination of land, capital, and labor. That would seem to lead to the question of how each of the three con-tributes to the value. His response is that the question is an absurdity, just like the question of which part of the child is derived from the father and which part from the mother. That is, there can be no answer to this type of absurd question. Von Wieser does not suggest that this means that there is no hope; rather, he insists that it is a practical mat-ter, likening it to a question of guilt—to what extent is someone guilty of committing a crime. Von Wieser grants that there are many varia-bles, but he maintains that just as a judge practically imputes, so does the economist. And, he reminds his readers that everyone imputes—when deciding to purchase a machine, he calculates how it will work and therefore how valuable it will be. He also reminds them that with-out the art of imputation there would be no business calculations and indeed no economy; just as without the art of legal imputation there would be no society (von Wieser 1901:111).

Von Wieser turned to each of the three parts of the economic con-dition. Labor has value because it is scarce—if no one ever needed to work, there would be virtually no difference between the rich man and the poor man because both could have everything they wanted without the need to toil, which von Wieser suggests would be a "Utopia" (von Wieser 1901: 113). Capital is next, and that means that with investing we are foregoing immediate profit for a longer term one. This leads to the theory of interest and von Wieser refers the reader to the "recent" translation of Böhm-Bawerk's *Capital and Interest* (von Wieser 1901: 115). Finally, von Wieser addresses the issue of value and maintains that value is a personal decision—that is, it is determined from a personal standpoint or what he calls "value in use." Each individual must decide how much that product will satisfy his need—regardless whether it is the rich man or the poor one (von Wieser 1901: 115–116, 119).

In 1911 Joseph Schumpeter was just beginning his career when von Wieser was at the apex of his. So, it is a testament of von Wieser's interest in the younger generation that he reviewed Schumpeter's *Das Wesen und der Hauptinhalt der theoretischen Nationalökonomik*. This was not a brief book review but was an extensive review essay. In the *Gesammelte Abhandlungen* it is 24 pages in length. Von Wieser allows that he is late to review Schumpeter's book and that it has already been considered by scholars of various positions—some have applauded Schumpeter while a few others have been critical—but von Wieser points out that the book has drawn much interest because of the richness of its content. Von Wieser admits that he will avoid going into the details of the book but does intend to examine Schumpeter's general theme. He takes it to be nothing less than an attempt to explicate the main theses of the theoretical national economics (von Wieser 1929b: 10–11). For this, Schumpeter deserves considerable praise. But in addition, Schumpeter is to be applauded because he does not simply offer snippets from the existing literature but is setting out the major ideas of the theoretical school. Schumpeter achieves this in two ways: first, by his enthusiasm, which combines scholarly precision with artistic freedom; second, by discussing the issues in a manner that it will encourage interest from many people. For von Wieser, the main question is whether Schumpeter was able to explain the fundamentals of the theoretical economics (von Wieser 1929b: 11). Von Wieser indicates that he and Schumpeter are members of the same Austrian School but that they differ in their methodological approaches. He suggests that Schumpeter believes that economics should be modeled on the natural sciences, which von Wieser denies. He notes that if Schumpeter is right, then he and his like-minded theoreticians are wrong. That is because Schumpeter's approach follows the objective view point of the natural sciences and rejects the Austrian emphasis on the subjectivity of value (von Wieser 1929b: 13). Many of the next several pages are devoted to von Wieser's objection to the natural science approach because it makes economics treat values as some object to be observed, whereas it is a psychological disposition which can only be inferred by certain observations. Furthermore, these types of observations cannot yield firm data that serves as the foundation for empirical theories. The natural sciences study physical objects, but the economist must be content to consider the actions prompted by consciousness. As such, the economist must be content with the limitations of imputation; something that the natural scientist does not need to contend with (von Wieser 1929b: 14–19). It is von Wieser's judgment that by aligning himself with the natural scientists and adopting their objective method that Schumpeter has failed to capture the essence and the main content of the theoretic economics. His method leads to hypotheses and speculation, thus away from the facts. In contrast, the psychological school remains committed to facts and drawing only the most warranted inferences from them. With facts, von Wieser keeps to what is known; with hypotheses, Schumpeter makes assumptions about the unknown. The psychological method does not tolerate hypotheses whereas they are necessary for the natural sciences to reach their final area (von Wieser 1929b: 20–22, 24–25).

Von Wieser delves into a few of Schumpeter's particular points to show where he is in error. Schumpeter fails to understand price because he does not comprehend value. In other words, Schumpeter's method prevented him from not just misunderstanding some of the basic ideas of economics, but that his approach led him to misinterpret the nature of theoretical economics (von Wieser 1929b: 30–31). In light of this, it is somewhat surprising that von Wieser's final evaluation of Schumpeter's book is extremely positive. He suggests that Schumpeter's main failure is that he feels that he has mastered everything. In von Wieser's opinion, that suggests that Schumpeter has not yet found the proper balance between too much and too little and that his youthful exuberance is the most praiseworthy of all mistakes because that is a symptom of a "strong power" ("starken Kraft") (von Wieser 1929b: 34).

In terms of von Wieser's works which are not devoted to value but reflects his overall thinking on theoretical economics, there is one final work to consider. That is von Wieser's contribution to Max Weber's *Grundriss der Sozialökonomik*. It is found in the first volume of Weber's multi-volume work, published in 1914. One way of considering von Wieser's work is to compare it to the other two contributions. The one by Karl Bücher deals with the developmental steps of economics: "Volkswirtschaftliche Entwicklingsstufen." It is a continuation of Bücher's theory of economic development and is extremely brief at 18 pages. The one by Joseph Schumpeter is also historically oriented:

"Epochen der Dogmen- und Methodengeschichte." Schumpeters's work is impressive with his accuracy and his insights and is just over 100 pages. In contrast, von Wieser has set his sights on theory: "Theorie der gesellschaftlichen Wirtschaft," and as his title indicates he was attempting to provide a theory of social economics. At almost 325 pages, it is more than an entry like Bücher's or even a monograph like Schumpeter's, but is a full-scale book. As such, it would require a major article to begin to do justice to it. In fact, the review essay written by the American economist Wesley C. Mitchell is 23 printed pages and even he admits that he did not do full justice to von Wieser's chapter (Mitchell 1917). But as will be shown shortly, Mitchell provided a scholarly and judicious appraisal of von Wieser's contribution.

Von Wieser's "Theorie der gesellschaftlichen Wirtschaft" is composed of a brief Introduction and four divisions or chapters. The introduction and the four chapters vary in length and that is indicated by the number of sections: the introduction has two sections (Sections 1, 2), the first chapter has 23 (Sections 3–25), the second chapter has 48 (Sections 26–74), the third chapter has three (Sections 78–80), the fourth chapter has five (§§ 81–85). Despite the shorter lengths of the introduction and chapters 3 and 4, those are of the greatest interest here.

The "Einleitung" ("Introduction") has two sections: the first one is devoted to von Wieser's methodology and the second explains the difference between his method and the mathematical one. He admits that the term "psychological" is not the best term to apply to his method because it is not "psychological" in the scientific sense of the word. That is, his method is not at all related to that which is known as the science of psychology. However, it is appropriate when one remembers that his method, like those of Menger and Böhm-Bawerk, is focused on the subjective. Von Wieser provides a carefully constructed account of his method. It is empirical and is based upon observation. It employs isolation and idealization. And, it functions according to a practice of abstraction. The result of this method is not a complete account of economics but is an increase in our understanding of economic processes. Thus, it partially shares in the methods of the natural sciences but does so without those sciences' reliance on mathematical formula (von Wieser 1914: 132–135, 137).

The first division is devoted to the "Theory of the Simple Economy" ("Theorie der Einfachen Wirtschaft") and in it von Wieser sets out the basic parts of the economy. Many of these are familiar from his other writings: the tripartite collection of land, labor, and capital, as well as the concept of the exchange of produced goods for money (von Wieser 1914: 167–170, 172–179, 180–184). And, part of this is his familiar use of "imputation" (von Wieser 1914: 206–215, 224–227). He concluded this division with the claim that economics is the study of how humans satisfy their needs and it utilizes the notions of supply and demand, calculation, and prediction. Each of these presupposes a sense of "value" ("Wert") which is why it is fundamental to von Wieser's entire thinking about economics (von Wieser 1914: 229–231).

The second division is on the "Theory of the People's Economy" ("Theorie der Volkswirtschaft") and it mostly deals with the single individual. This does not mean that there is only one person in terms of economics; von Wieser makes it plain that economics involves at least two individuals. In section 30 von Wieser discusses "exchange" ("Tausch") which he defines as the oversupplied against the necessary. If someone has far more of something than he needs, then that something has little or no "utility value" ("Nutzwert"). Accordingly, the individual is eager to exchange what he has but does not need for that which he needs but does not have. The two people involved in this exchange is what von Wieser refers to as an "exchange pair" ("Tauschpaar") (von Wieser 1914: 245–247). He then discussed how the exchange moved from a private one to a market one and that involved the need to determine prices. And, the price was determined by the supply but especially by the demand, which involves the "exchange value" ("Tauschwert"). Von Wieser maintained that there was a personal or subjective "exchange value" as well as an objective "exchange value." He suggested that the best means to explain a subjective "exchange value" is to consider money. Money is what everyone values, but not for what it is, but for what it does. In this sense, having a large supply of money is not terribly valuable because it is not doing anything. It is only when one exchanges money for goods that it is used and has personal value. Although von Wieser does not explicitly state it, he seems to reject the idea that there actually could be an objective "exchange value"—there can only be what the individual believes is valuable to him or to her (von Wieser 1914: 286–291). The remainder of the division is devoted to specific parts of economics: money, labor, and profit. Some of the latter is historical and some is contemporary—for example, the classical liberal economics of non-intervention which was superseded by the state's duty to protect women and children with labor laws and for helping to ensure a balance between the workers and the large industries (von Wieser 1914: 410–414).

The third division expands the discussion of the economic process from concentrating on the individual to the involvement of the state: "Theory of the State Economy" ("Theorie der Staatswirtschaft"). It is just fifteen pages in length but von Wieser makes three major points. First, it is important to recognize that the state economy is not entirely distinct from the private economy. However, the two differ in terms of income—for the private economy it is derived from labor and exchange, but for the state it is from taxes and duties. Yet, there are some similarities when it comes to the railroad and the postal service. But there are other parts of the state that do not directly participate in economic exchange, yet are institutions which regulate that. These are the courts, offices, and administrative faculties which govern economic exchange. The state does not participate directly in the economic process but it does aid that process (von Wieser 1914: 415–417). The state has an additional duty and that is to care for the poor and the needy—indeed for the general welfare of the citizens. Then there is a further obligation which is to maintain internal order and secure safety from external aggressors. In other words, the state does not exist for itself but for its people (von Wieser 1914: 417).

This emphasis on the collective does not mean that von Wieser thought that the state somehow transcended the individual. Rather, the state exists to further the interests of the many individuals. That involves promoting everything from the most basic of human needs to the highest regions of culture. Just as an individual will have private insurance for his house, the state acts as insurance for its citizens. But again, von Wieser insisted that the state does not replace the individual, but helps the individual achieve the best possible life (von Wieser 1914: 418).

Von Wieser did not refer to many sources but he did offer two: Friedrich List for his theory of productive powers and Hermann Heinrich Gossen on the law of satiation. These two nineteenth century political economists were rather different: List was regarded as a forerunner of the German Historical School because of his promotion of duties and tariffs. Gossen was considered a major figure who helped formulate the Austrian School's preoccupation with the individual. But von Wieser had no problem in making use of those ideas which helped explain modern economics. If Gossen discussed how individual needs can be satisfied, List provided an account of those public means which contribute to those satisfactions; namely, railroads and the postal service (von Wieser 1914: 418–419). While it may not seem that these means immediately affect economics, von Wieser argued that it is the street car which conveys the worker to the factory and it is the post office which delivers the mail from the sender to the receiver. Hence, the state or the city provides the services which help economic exchanges to take place (von Wieser 1914: 420–421).[7]

The fourth and final division expands the economic process even further—the "Theory of the World Economics" ("Theorie der Weltwirtschaft"). In contrast to the section on the state where von Wieser referred only to two other scholars, in this section he mentions (though does not refer to) more than 15 scholars in his literature list. And he notes how the world economy differs from the state economy. The state economy serves to protect the social order and ensures that individual interests do not overpower the general good. The state economy also administrates the public means of exchange and transportation. It is a unified economy with its basis in its state capital. It brings together all classes from the peasants, to the workers, to the cultured and educated people. The state is the highest organ (von Wieser 1914: 426–427). In the world economy this highest organ is missing; there is no capital and there is no sense of unity. In its place is the desire for foreign products and that involves determining the price of those goods and the cost of acquiring them from abroad. Von Wieser recognized the importance of these factors but he did not provide any real answers to them. Instead, he concluded with a few brief observations regarding the doctrine of free trade and issue of trade balances. The Mercantilists rejected free trade in favor of protectionism, but the classical liberals promoted trade. The modern world economy is a combination of the two, and von Wieser noted that the richness or the poorness of the country tended to influence how much trade freedom or trade protection there is. And he also observes that the central bank plays a role in how much trade there is by influencing both the reserves that a country has and by manipulating the currency exchange. He closes with some additional comments on List's theory of national protection and suggests that the Germans may have struck the right balance between free trade and national protection. But rather than discussing this, he concludes that it is necessary to break off his theoretical investigation in order to offer room for others (von Wieser 1914: 440–444). One has the sense that von Wieser was well aware that he had gone far beyond what Max Weber had wanted when he assigned him the work on theory. And, one also has the sense that as much as von Wieser was interested in the economics of the state and the individual, he did not have much interest in examining the economics of the international community. That may have been because his concern was always with economic theory and not with international law. Laws were the basis for the juridical, but value was critical to the Austrian economists. Before turning to von Wieser's theory of value, it is fitting to close with a brief account of a remarkable review of von Wieser's contribution to Weber's Grundriss der Sozialökonomik.

Wesley C. Mitchell's "Wieser's Theory of Social Economics" is well worth discussing because he was an educated and impartial appraiser of von Wieser's work and was well-suited to offer a careful evaluation of it. He briefly mentioned how Weber's Grundriss der Sozialökonomik was intended to replace the old Handbuch compiled by Gustav Schönberg.[8] Mitchell also noted that it was a "piquant triumph" that the "editors" (sic) chose von Wieser and Schumpeter because as Schumpeter had pointed out, the methods of the Austrian School were "bitterly contested in Germany, and whose disciples were long barred from German professorships" (Mitchell 1917: 95).

Mitchell remarked that von Wieser's prestige in his work was not only derived from its position in the literature but from his remarkable contribution to the theory of social economics. He suggested that it was similar to Mill's Political Economy in that both works were "elegant in proportions, mature in expression and authoritative in source." However, Mitchell insisted that this comparison with Mill does not do justice to von Wieser because the latter's work is the first systematic treatise on theory authored by the Austrians, whereas Mill had built upon others. And, Mitchell insisted that von Wieser's work was far more original than Mill's. Finally, Mill wrote on many different subjects but von Wieser had spent a lifetime on these considerations. Mitchell's initial opinion is that this "is the fruition of a lifetime's reflection as well as the crowning achievement of a famous school" (Mitchell 1917: 95–96). Since, unfortunately, it had not been reviewed in the two and a half years since it was published, Mitchell provided "a rather full account of the book."

Mitchell noted that von Wieser was mostly in agreement with the classical school but he broke with it when it came to the role of the state. In contrast to the classical doctrine of non-interference, von Wieser argued that the state needed to intervene in order to prevent "economic freedom from breeding economic oppression" and that it was necessary to "protect the commonweal against the despotic might of capital" (Mitchell 1917: 108).

Mitchell concluded with the admission that while he found von Wieser's work fascinating, what he found most remarkable was his attitude regarding his own work. Although there had been massive changes since von Wieser published his first book in 1884, he had not changed his thinking. Mitchell wrote: "We know that he holds fast to the fundamentals of his youth; but how does he justify that attitude?" (Mitchell 1917: 108). Von Wieser believed that he was justified because of his method, but Mitchell complained that despite his claim that his method is one of observation, he does not do that in practice. For Mitchell, von Wieser's claim to use the psychological method is misleading, not only because that makes it seem that economics is dependent on psychology but because von Wieser does not deal with economic activity as it is, but "as it ought to be." That means that his work is not a positive theory but a normative one (Mitchell 1917: 109–113). And, that means that the discipline of economics needs to take psychology more seriously than von Wieser did. Mitchell advises that economics needs to make a fresh start by examining economic behavior. Von Wieser banned the aids most helpful in this endeavor: "psychological analysis, historical research and statistical measurements" (Mitchell 1917: 117–118). Mitchell may have been right about this, but then his economic work would have no resemblance to that of von Wieser.[9] Von Wieser was not interested in measuring what consumers do; he investigated their motives. That is why the theme which runs through his work is the issue of "value" ("Wert").

Von Wieser on Value

Friedrich von Wieser was preoccupied with the issue of "value" ("Wert") for almost his entire scholarly life. It is a major focus of a previously unpublished work from the year 1876 to the article "Theorie des Geldes" for the *Handwörterbuch der Staatswissenschaften* which he had finished shortly before his death in July 1926 (von Wieser 1927). This focus is found in numerous articles but especially in his two major books. The first one is *Über den Ursprung und die Hauptgesetze des wirthschaftliche Werthes* which was published in 1884 and the second one is *Der natürliche Werth* which appeared in 1889.[10] The first book on the origin and the main laws of economic values was published while von Wieser was a "Privatdozent" while the second book on natural value appeared after he had become a professor. Both set out in more detail some of the ideas found in his early work "Über das Verhältnis der Kosten zum Wert."[11] Yet, the early writing is worth some consideration because it dealt with the interconnection between value and time and between production and cost.

Von Wieser began by indicating that he saw his task as investigating the connection between costs and values or the influence of production on costs. He repeated the claim that when there is an overabundance of something then it has little or no value. We may value what we possess but we also place a value on what we do not have but need. We have no need to produce the goods that we already have in sufficient quantities but we need to produce those that we need. This is not simply a matter of production but an issue of the time frame from production to the satisfaction of needs (von Wieser 1929d: 377). He uses as an example a Canadian hunter who is in need of killing an animal to get the fur in order to make clothing that will protect him from the approaching winter's cold. Thus, he is in immediate need of this. If he happens to make a second piece of clothing, he may consider it somewhat valuable as a reserve. But he has no use for a third article of clothing so it has no value to him. For a second example, von Wieser wrote about a man who lives a simple life and has enough food for now and for the immediate future. For him, more food or food of a higher quality has no use for him; hence, has no value. Finally, von Wieser wrote about an art collector who specializes in rare paintings. For him, another painting gives him no more pleasure and has little value. Von Wieser's point in these three examples is that there is a hierarchy of goods corresponding to a hierarchy of needs. The Canadian hunter has the greatest need; the simple man has less; and the art collector has virtually no need what so ever (von Wieser 1929d: 378–379). Or, as he put it a bit later: the significance of the need is there as long as there is a need—with the implication that there is no significance if there is no need (von Wieser 1929d: 383).

Von Wieser then turned to the issue of time. If we have sufficient goods, then the need for time is mostly irrelevant. Time is critical if we do not have the goods and need to produce them immediately. And, the value of the goods is largely dependent on how soon we need it (von Wieser 1929d: 390–391, 394). That value in turn influences the price we are willing to pay and that the price that the producer wants and the price that the consumer will pay is up to negotiation (von Wieser 1929d: 400). From this, von Wieser concludes that rather than price being the final ground of value, it is value that is the final ground of the price.[12] Thus, the price of an object is not the defining characteristic; but it is that thing's value that actually is that definitional character (von Wieser 1929d: 404).

In the "Vorwort" to *Über den Ursprung und die Hauptgesetze des wirthschaftlichen Werthes* von Wieser acknowledged his indebtedness to Menger for prompting him to recognize the importance of value in economics (von Wieser 1884: VII). He followed Menger's approach in so far as he discussed the "concept and essence of value" ("Begriff und Wesen des Werthes"). However, von Wieser departed from his teacher by emphasizing the importance of language in economics in general and, specifically, in regard to the concept of value.

Über den Ursprung und die Hauptgesetze des wirthschaftlichen Werthes has a preface, four major divisions, and a conclusion. Both the preface and the conclusion are brief while the first three sections are about 40 pages each. The fourth section differs from the previous three by being almost double the size. The first section is, as noted, devoted to the concept and essence of value and so it is primarily methodological in orientation. As a theorist, von Wieser was heavily invested in the use of method, but as a theoretical economist he had massive complaints about the dominant methodology—that of the natural sciences. His complaint was that scientists study phenomena so that the language they use reflects what they study. As a result, no one takes issue with what the scientist states because he is only reflecting how one responds to physical phenomena. But linguistic use is different for the human sciences and that is because those sciences must consider a situation from a specific point of view. Von Wieser offers the example of someone's death—for a non-jurist, it is a death but for a jurist it may very well be a matter of murder. The natural sciences are the realm of discoveries but von Wieser suggests that the human sciences belong to the area of interpretation. He points to the various approaches to the true, the good, and the beautiful (von Wieser 1884: 1–7). Turning to the concept of value, he suggested that it had two versions—an objective one and a subjective one. It is the objective version of value that is the more common one and it is the belief that value somehow is inherent in the object. In this view, it is the object that gives the value. This prompted von Wieser to remark that there is an impersonal value and a personal one and that the objective concept of value is the impersonal one and that the subjective notion of value is the personal one. He recognized that the common way of speaking about value made it difficult for people to recognize that value was personal and subjective. He stressed that it cannot be emphasized enough that value is a subjective thing.[13] He admits that the "personal concept of value" ("persönlicher Werthbegriff") has both form and content and while the former is objective, the latter is subjective. The problem is our tendency to conflate the two into something objective. He uses the example of a gold coin to explain this tendency—we consider the value of the coin to be dependent on the color, the brightness, and the weight of the coin. These are all measurable factors so it seems reasonable to assume that they determine the value of the coin. However, von Wieser takes issue with this by pointing to a counterfeit coin—it apparently has the same characteristics of the genuine coin in that it has the same color, shine, and weight. But those who recognize it as a counterfeit assign no value to it. Von Wieser's point is that value is not inherent in the coin but in our subjective evaluation of it (von Wieser 1884: 12–13).

Von Wieser was fully cognizant of the difficulty of his task to explain the subjective roots of value. He suggested that the subjective concept of value is without doubt difficult to understand but is true. In contrast, the objective concept of value is easily and comfortably comprehended, even though it is wrong. He noted that people think that value is like a price; and since everyone knows what the price of something is, then they think that they also know its value. He concluded that the impersonal value is regarded as a value for all; i.e., "objective" value.[14] The issue is how to overcome this conviction that value is objective. Von Wieser suggested that his preliminary approach would be discussed in four historical steps. But before outlining the four steps, he reminded his readers that the question "What is value?" ("Was ist der Werth?") cannot be easily answered and that the notion of value needed to be carefully defined. While definitions are always helpful, given the common, but erroneous, concept of value, it is even more imperative that his definition be as clear as possible (von Wieser 1884: 32–33). The first step was with the Mercantilists and the Physiocrats and that the former believed that value resided in the metal, whereas the latter suggested that it resided in the coin. Both views were widespread and both were fundamentally wrong about value. The second step was that of Adam Smith and it is to his credit that he drew attention to the notion of value. Unfortunately, he and his school promoted the most impersonal notion of value that was then so widely accepted. The third step was undertaken by German professors and it is to their honor that they insisted that Smith's notion of impersonal value was incorrect and a correct one would need to recognize the need for empirical facts to accompany theory. The fourth and last step is the one in which the attempt at understanding the concept of value has been replaced by the recognition of the importance of the "subjective act of estimating value" ("subjective Act der Werthschätzung") (von Wieser 1884: 32–35). These four historical steps lead to von Wieser's own attempt to explain what value is.

Von Wieser saw his task as explaining how from the many various interests that we have can we arrive at the actual impelling interest? In this, von Wieser acknowledged that he was following in the footsteps of the theoretical school but he insisted that "they" (Menger) had not paid enough attention to the linguistic side and how it reflected our psychological ideas about interests. Thus, "they" minimized the empirical for the theoretical and it was von Wieser's indication that he would focus both on the theoretical and the practical (von Wieser 1884: 36–41).

The second main section begins with a warning that there is no hope for understanding a tool unless one knows about the objects the tool is to be used on and what the intended use of the tool is. The tool here is "value estimating" ("Werthschätzung"), the objects are goods, and the intended use of the tool is to aid in understanding the value of the goods (von Wieser 1884: 42). It is relatively easy to define goods since they are the means to actually satisfy needs ("Mittel der Bedürfnissbefriedigung") and that it is also relatively easy to define in terms of economics what these goods are. They are things that are not simply useful for satisfying needs, but are recognized by us as actually having the potential to do so. Thus, it is not merely a matter of supply, but one of demand (von Wieser 1884: 42–43). Unfortunately, most of the focus has been on the supply side of the issue and that was indicated by the concern with the rarity or the deficiency of a thing. Von Wieser pointed to Malthus and Darwin and their notions of overpopulation and struggle which led to the fight over scarce goods. But he also pointed out that descriptions of primitive cultures seemed to over emphasize the struggle for sustenance. In modern times, the stress seems to be on production of goods (von Wieser 1884: 43–55). Like Menger, von Wieser spends considerable time on production processes and ordering. Like Menger, he does so because he realizes that most economists are preoccupied with production of goods because those are issues which can be calculated and objectively evaluated. But as with Menger, von Wieser's interest lays in the subjectivity of valuing. That is connected to the issue of use, so value and use are the main subjects of the third main section.

Von Wieser begins the third main section by reminding his readers that he has established that value is determined by human interest and that goods have no value if people have no interest in them. As a result, the origin of value is bound up with the interest in acquiring particular goods (von Wieser 1884: 79). Furthermore, one has interest in those things that he needs and can use. Von Wieser offers the example of a man in the desert. He comes across some water which he desperately needs. Like all humans, he values that which keeps his body functioning and in this case the water is even more precious because without it, he would lose his life (von Wieser 1884: 81). Von Wieser connects the greater the need with the greater the value (von Wieser 1884: 82–85, 89, 92–93). Von Wieser moves from his doctrine that the use of something determines its value to the two other issues: cost and labor. He dismisses the notion that the cost of something determines its value on the grounds that it is not the cost of something which interests us; rather, it is our need for it. If we do not need it, then the cost is irrelevant (von Wieser 1884: 98–103). Von Wieser is slightly more sympathetic to those who connect value with labor and he reminds us that the labor-value connection is not just a contemporary idea but was found in the theories of Adam Smith and David Ricardo (von Wieser 1884: 105–106). Von Wieser admits that our language suggests that something's value rests upon the cost of producing it but that it is not labor that gives something its value; rather, it is our use for it. As with all cost theories, the cost of "labor theory" ("Arbeitstheorie") is replaced by the "theory of use-value" ("Theorie des Nutzwerthes") (von Wieser 1884: 118–120).

The fourth main section has the title "Die Hauptregeln der Werthschätzung" ("The Major Rules of Value Estimating") and von Wieser's first step in this section is to determine the highest rule. He reminds us that it is irrelevant to inquire about the source of something or ask about the size of the thing. Nor is it pertinent to think about the value of something if there is a large amount of it. These are important economic questions but are not germane to determining the value of some object. What is germane is the specific need for a specific object and recognizing both the need and the assumption that that object will satisfy that desire. Furthermore, the person needs to believe that the object is available in sufficient quantity and sufficient quality to satisfy that need. These observations may lead one to think that von Wieser was only concerned with one thing and that is its use and value. But he makes it very plain that a person who is evaluating something is also keeping in mind what he already possesses and those other things that he needs. Ignoring these considerations leads to numerous misunderstandings and errors (von Wieser 1884: 121–124). In von Wieser's view, much of the problem is caused by people not understanding the correlation of objects to needs. To help clarify, he provides an example of an individual who is crossing a desert. If he has one set of rations, then he has secured his life. If he has two sets of rations, then he will have added strength. If he has three sets, then he can relax knowing that he has far more than he needs. If he has a fourth, then he can afford to give them to his horse. This notion of the number of goods and the needs leads him to his doctrine of marginal utility ("Grenznutzen") and he allows that it is similar if not identical to Jevons "final degree of utility" (von Wieser 1884: 126–128). But his main point is that value cannot be separated from use (von Wieser 1884: 131–135). This fourth main section is the lengthiest in large part because von Wieser returns to the issues of production and cost. It is only toward the end that he takes up the question about value and its relation to use. Value is not only estimated for its practical use, it is also measured and evaluated. Once again, the question is how much of a need does one have for this particular good? Von Wieser admits that this is a subjective and a psychological issue so it is resistant to a firm answer based upon observation. However, we are to draw some inferences based upon what we see and hear regarding the intensity of the interest (von Wieser 1884: 180–183). However, he does not overestimate how difficult it is to read someone—even one's self: "How difficult it is for humans to understand themselves!" ("Wie schwer sich doch die Menschen selbst verstehen!") (von Wieser 1884: 190).

Von Wieser concludes his book on the origins of the notion of value by pointing out that he had demonstrated that the estimation of a value of something was tied to our belief that it was of use to us. The more we believe we need something, the more we assign value to it. Thus, value is related to our interest in it. He ends with the claim that he has shown that value estimating was not a weapon that one human used against another. Rather, it was a weapon that humans used in their economic struggles with nature.[15]

Von Wieser's second book on value was published in 1889. By this time, he had been promoted from a "Privatdozent" in Vienna to full professor in Prague. But the theme of the book was still value and he was concerned that readers might think that it was a repetition of the origins book. In the "Vorwort" he insisted that it was not merely a repetition of ideas found in his earlier book but was almost an entirely new book. Only some of the fundamental principles remained the same.[16] But one crucial difference was that the 1889 book was divided into two main sections. The first part which makes up almost the entire book is devoted to the notion of value in the private economy, whereas the much shorter second part is focused on the concept of value as it is found in the state's economy. The second part is only 30 pages and has only five numbered paragraphs (Sections 62–66) while the first part is slightly more than 200 pages and contains 61 numbered paragraphs (Sections 1–61).

The first section of *Natürliche Werth* differed from the earlier book by launching into a discussion of the elementary theory of value instead of an account of linguistic usage. Von Wieser reminds us that not everything has value—things that are in superabundance have no value; only those things that we both need and are in short supply (von Wieser 1889: 1–4). However, von Wieser also distinguishes between those desires and needs which are economical and those which are not. Those desires or needs for vanity, artistic appreciation, or moral standards are no doubt needs, but they are not economic needs. In contrast, economic needs are satisfied by various goods and so we assign value to those goods. He further reminds us that there is a limit or boundary where something that has been satisfying a need and then begins to become something that is not only not needed, but is now regarded as something bad. Von Wieser uses the example of people who have been craving some food but when they begin to have too much of it, it begins to make them ill. The point is that too little and too much are unpleasant situations, what satisfies us is determined by us to be the right amount for us. Furthermore, the need is determined by a specific time frame—some needs only need to be satisfied occasionally while others are recurring needs. Von Wieser is thinking specifically of the recurrent need for nourishment (von Wieser 1889: 5–7). These points prompt him to discuss "scales of satisfaction" ("Sättigungs-Scalen") but he warns that such scales can only be approximate because they will change with different people and even within the same person, at different times. The determining measure will be the use of a good. Thus, economics is not simply to correlation between supply and demand, but the specific need for something for that person at that time (von Wieser 1889: 10–11).

Nature may be bountiful but rarely is the bounty so plentiful that every satisfaction can be achieved. Von Wieser argues that most often we must be content with the slightest satisfaction of our needs. This is what Gossen had called "value of the last atom," Jevons had referred to as "final degree of utility," and von Wieser has named "marginal utility." He noted with some satisfaction that his "Grenznutzen" has been widely accepted (von Wieser 1889: 12). He reminds us again that something has value if we can use it; that which is in abundance has no specific use and hence no particular value. He points out that everything is more than plentiful in paradise; accordingly, there is no want, no goods, and no value. But here on earth there is a scarcity of goods and a corresponding large number of needs. These are goods that in Menger's terminology "value goods" ("Güterwerth") (von Wieser 1889: 20). As von Wieser points out, these goods have value because they have use. The next question us how to estimate the value of a single good. He suggests that there is a general worth as well as a specific value and his concern is with the latter. The former may be of some theoretic interest but it the latter is important for practical matters. He offers as an example an individual who has two pieces of bread but needs only one to satisfy his hunger. In one sense, the second piece of bread has no immediate value; however, in another sense it does if the individual gives it to someone who needs it and has asked for it (von Wieser 1889: 23–24).

Von Wieser insists again that the highest principle of all economics is use.[17] And, he insists that if there is some conflict between value and use, it is use that is to be regarded as the most important. He helps clarify this by pointing out that where there is abundance, it is difficult to determine value, but where there is scarcity, it is easier to determine value (von Wieser 1889: 33–36). The next issue for von Wieser is to distinguish between what he calls "exchange value" ("Verkehrswerth") and "natural value" ("natürlicher Werth"). The first can be regarded in a subjective sense as well as an objective one. Von Wieser begins to explain both by pointing to the fact that a person who can buy and then sell something produces a new impulse in the single economy and it does so in the sense of its "use value" ("Gebrauchswerth"). But before explaining that, he notes that money is regarded as a good by everyone because of its exchange value (von Wieser 1889: 45). However, von Wieser argues that money is not nearly as important as the goods which money can purchase. He illustrates this by pointing to a poor man who values his winter coat. Its value does not reside in its monetary worth but in the fact that it is the thing that can keep him warm in the cold weather. If he were to lose it, it would not be the loss of its monetary value that would affect him but the loss of the protection from the elements. Von Wieser adds that the rich man will not be so bothered by its loss because he can easily buy a new one to replace the lost one. In contrast, the poor man will be extremely troubled by its loss because he cannot afford to buy a replacement. Thus, it is not money that determines value, but its use. It is in this sense that we can talk of the subjective sense of the use value. And, he adds that it is amazing that for the most part this notion of subjective use has largely been unnoticed. It is to Menger's credit that he was the first one to have drawn attention to it and this attention was not the least of what he has accomplished (von Wieser 1889: 46–48).

Von Wieser now turns to the objective sense of use value. It is typical for economists to think of this use as something that can be determined objectively. That is why they are so eager to ascribe such importance to money and to price—in the belief that this reflects the impersonal aspect of exchange. It is also why economists place such emphasis on production and why socialists place such importance on labor. Von Wieser spends the remainder of this section discussing Marxist economics before returning to the notion of value in the third section.

It is in this section that von Wieser employs one of his most important conceptual tools and that is the notion of "calculation" ("Zurechnung"). Once again, he emphasizes the personal and subjective side of this because the individual must calculate the value of something for his own use (von Wieser 1889: 67). People tend to ascribe value to land, capital, and work but as he argues, these have little or no value by themselves but gain it through their use. In other words, unfelled trees in a forest, pasture that is neglected, or too much water in a stream has no intrinsic value, but each becomes valuable once it is needed. But von Wieser insists that if time is involved, so it is not only a matter of what a thing's value is to someone right now; it is especially important in the sense of expected future use. Hence, the importance of calculating for satisfying future needs (von Wieser 1889: 68–72).

It was Menger who previously was the one who began to express the appreciation for the importance of "Zurechnung," but it was a minor part of his theory of value. Since his notion of value was not as important to his overall theory of subjective value, von Wieser suggested that he did not feel the need to have developed it more. It is von Wieser's task to do this (von Wieser 1889: 80–84). To aid in understanding the notion of "Zurechnung" von Wieser offers two examples. In the first, a hunter is being threatened by a wild animal and he has only one bullet left. There is no reason to try to do any calculation: either he successfully uses his last bullet to kill the attacking animal and thus lives or he misses the shot and will undoubtedly be killed by the animal. In the second example, von Wieser suggests that there is an artist who seeks recognition so he needs to think not just about the design of the leaded vessel that he intends to create but also calculate how much of each ingredient that he should use (von Wieser 1889: 85–86). In both cases, what the people have in their possession is important. However, so is the calculation of what they will need, how much effort that must go into it, what sort of cost should be given to it, and so on. Each of these are in need of calculation and only by arriving at the most accurate is one able to gain the most profit or value from it (von Wieser 1889: 91–92, 110–112).

The fourth section can be dispensed with rather quickly because it is von Wieser's discussion of the natural value of land, capital, and labor. Land is not worth much if it is not used; its value is connected with its fruits (von Wieser 1889: 153–155). It is slightly different with labor but that is because socialists contend that all value is determined by labor. But von Wieser points out that it is not labor itself that is valuable, but the product that labor has produced (von Wieser 1889: 156–160). Von Wieser concludes this section with a continuation of its beginnings, and that is with a focus on capital. He had begun with the announcement that the concept of capital produces the greatest confusion because it is the most difficult to explain. But von Wieser does not so much offer an explanation as he does a response to Böhm-Bawerk. Hence, a discussion of von Wieser's notion of capital will be addressed in the next chapter in the section on capital (von Wieser 1889: 132–133, 162–163).

In the final section von Wieser turns to examining what he refers to as "communal economies" ("Gemeinwirthschaften") and he notes that there are many different forms of these. However, he restricts his examination to only the most important one and that is the "state economy" ("Staatwirthschaft"). He suggests that because the focus has traditionally been on the private economy, the investigation into a theory of the state economy is in its beginning stages. As a result, he will restrict his comments to two major areas: income economy (or finance economy) and expenditure (or state administration). The problem was that the economists who did discuss the state economy did so in the belief that it was similar to the private economy. So, any rules applying to the private economy were presupposed to apply to the state economy as well. In the opinion of Adam Smith and his school, when they talked about value in the state economy they invariably meant "exchange value." And, that is a large reason why Smith and his followers were such believers in free trade. The greater the freedom to engage in trade, the greater the income for business people and also the state. Thus, the state was dependent upon business in order to fill the state's coffers (von Wieser 1889: 209–211). In Germany, that belief in free trade was questioned by Friedrich List. He argued that "exchange value" is useful in discussing private economies but is not fully appropriate when investigating state economies. For List, it was important to realize that tariffs and taxes are not only important measures for states to introduce but they also serve to differentiate the state economy from a private one. Von Wieser concludes his historical overview with a few comments on the then recently deceased Emil Sax. Perhaps even more than List, Sax believed that political economy had to involve the state economy (von Wieser 1889: 211–213).

Concluding Comments

Friedrich von Wieser continued to emphasize the subjective side of economics, especially in his examination of value.[18] But he was increasingly tempted to depart from Menger and to think about economics in more than the subjective sense. Unlike Menger, and even unlike Böhm-Bawerk, von Wieser was moving more in the direction of Max Weber and his notion of social economics. Von Wieser was more than happy to credit Menger for beginning the Austrian School of Economics. He was more than willing to credit Böhm-Bawerk and to admit that he had learned much from his writings. While his own reputation rested mainly on his work on value, von Wieser noted that he shared much of this reputation with his brother-in-law.

Notes

1 Although he is regarded as an economic theorist, he never thought of people as just economic actors. In his six lectures published under the title *Recht und Macht*, von Wieser spoke of how important it is for an economic theorist to understand that man is more than a "homo

oeconomicus." He explained that the same year that he had published his book on value, he was reading Tolstoy and Turgeniev whose works helped reinforce the idea that humans have desires and weaknesses and are living beings. von Wieser 1919: 18.

2   The contrast between this Palgrave entry and Bonar's earlier article in the *Quarterly Journal of Economics* is remarkable. In "The Austrian Economists and their View on Value" Bonar provided a rather complete and positive review of Menger's, von Wieser's, and Böhm-Bawerk's theories and showed a sophisticated understanding of the Austrian's emphasis on subjective value. If Bonar's 1888 article has any drawback, it is his preference for invoking Jevons. Bonar 1888. Von Wieser does not comment on Bonar's article but he does refer to his 1888 article. von Wieser 1926: 817. But in his 1901 article "The Austrian School and the Theory of Value" he referred to Bonar's article as an "excellent essay." von Wieser 1901: 108.

3   In von Wieser's view, the Manchester school believed in unrestricted freedom in economics, as well as in almost every other area. He wrote that they held that "All that which must not be unconditionally prohibited, should therefore be permitted."("Alles, was nicht unbedingt verboten werden müßte, solle daher erlaubt sein."). He also took issue with Herbert Spencer's insistence that it was man against the state. Instead of the individual against the state, von Wieser maintained that it was the "social powers of the citizens against the social power of the state ("In der Volkswirtschaft steht nicht der Mann gegen den Staat, sondern gesellschftliche Mächte der Bürger gegen die gesellschaftliche Macht des Staates."). Note that the citizens have a plurality of powers as opposed to the single power of the state. von Wieser 1919: 132, 139, 140.

4   The article "Final Degree of Utility" that von Wieser referred to was written by a General F. A. Walker, who was the late president of M.I.T. His focus was almost entirely on Jevons, and Menger and the Austrians are only mentioned in passing. Walker 1926: 59–61. It seems odd that von Wieser does not at least mention his article "Grenznutzen," which appeared in the second and third editions of the *Handwörterbuch der Staatswissenschaften*. This article is reprinted in von Wieser 1929a.

5   Von Wieser does not provide an indication of where this theory of income is found, and it is not evident that it existed.

6   It appeared in the March 1891 issue of *The Economic Journal*. There is a version in von Wieser's *Gesammelte Abhandlungen* that was a German translation of the English original. von Wieser 1929c.

7   Von Wieser complained that the theory of the state economy is mostly neglected so he praised List for discussing it in his *Nationale System der Politischen Oekonomie*. Although List may not have been completely correct in his account of tariffs as a means for national protection, he did take the matter seriously. von Wieser 1914: 422, 424.

8   Mitchell 1917: 95. For an account of Weber's role in the change from the *Handbuch* to the *Grundriss* see Adair-Toteff 2021: 83–89 and 92–103.

9   In his Foreword to the English translation of von Wieser's *Grundriss* contribution, Mitchell did not alter his high opinion of the work. In fact, he uses some of the same lines of praise that he had employed a decade previously. If anything, the early criticism is gone and is replaced with clear and obvious admiration. Mitchell 1927: ix, xii.

10 A remainder that I use the spelling of the original so a modern spelling of the title would be *Über den Ursprung und die Hauptgesetze des wirtschaftlichen Werthes.*

11 Von Hayek justified including this as an appendix to von Wieser's *Gesammelte Abhandlungen* on the grounds that it represented von Wieser's position on value. von Hayek admitted that it may have lost some of its relevance, yet it was critical in understanding von Wieser's theory of value. von Hayek 1929: XXXIV.

12 "Damit soll aber keinwegs gesagt sein, daß der Preis der letzte Grund des Wertes ist. Umgekehrt ist der Wert der letzte Grund des Preises." von Wieser 1929d: 402.

13 "Der Satz, dass der Werth in Wahrheit eine subjective Erscheinung sei, kann nicht eindringlich genug gefasst werden." von Wieser 1884: 10–11.

14 "So wird der unpersönliche Werth zum Werth für Alle, zum 'objectiven" Werth." von Wieser 1884: 11–13, 19.

15 "Wir haben hiemit gezeigt, dass die Gabe der Werthschätzung ursprünglich nicht eine Waffe des einen Menschen wider den andern, sondern eine gemeinsame Ausstattung Aller im wirthschaftlichen Kampfe wider die Nature ist." von Wieser 1884: 214.

16 "Das Buch ist demnach keinwegs eine Wiederholung des ersten, sondern eine durchwegs neue, zum grössten Theile ganz neue Gegenstände betreffende Arbeit, die nur die allgemeinen Grundsätze mit jenem gemein hat." von Wieser 1889: XI.

17 "Das *oberste Princip aller Wirthschaft is der Nutzen.*" von Wieser 1889: 32–33.

18 One economics scholar who understood and appreciated von Wieser's contribution to the theory of value was William Smart. He had translated two of Böhm-Bawerk's books and was more than familiar with the early Austrian School's views on value. In *An Introduction to the Theory of Value* he made no claim to originality and indicated that his theory was first developed by Menger and Jevons and then worked out by von Wieser and Böhm-Bawerk. In particular, he singled out von Wieser's *natürliche Werth.* Smart had first published this work in 1891 and then wrote a Preface to the second edition of 1910. Smart 1966: ix–x, 32.

References

Adair-Toteff, C. (2021) *Max Weber's Path from Political Economics to Social Economics.* Abingdon: Routledge.

Bonar, J. (1888) "The Austrian Economists and their View of Value." *Quarterly Review of Economics.* October (1888) Issue. 1–32.

Bonar, J. (1926) "The Austrian School of Economists." In Higgens H. (ed.), *Palgrave's Dictionary of Political Economy.* Vol. I. A–E. London: Macmillan and Co. 73.

Hayek, F. A. von (1929) "Friedrich Freiherr von Wieser." In *Gesammelte Abhandlungen.* Mit einer Biographischen Einleitung. Herausgegeben von Friedrich A. von Hayek. Tübingen: Verlag von J.C.B. Mohr (Paul Siebeck). V–XXII.

Mitchell, W.C. (1917) "Wieser's Theory of Social Economics." *Political Science Quarterly*. Vol. 32. No. 1 (Mar., 1917). 95–118.

Mitchell, W.C. (1927) "Foreword." *Social Economics*. By Friedrich von Wieser. Translated by A. Ford Hinrichs. With a Preface by Wesley Clair Mitchell. New York: Adelphi Co.

Smart, W. (1966) *An Introduction to the Theory of Value*. New York: Augustus M. Kelley. Publishers.

Walker, F.A. (1926) "Final Degree of Utility." In Higgens H. (ed.), *Palgrave's Dictionary of Political Economy*. Vol. II. F–M. London: Macmillan and Co. 59–61.

Wieser, F. von (1884) *Ursprung und Hauptgesetze des wirtschaftliche Werthes*. Wien: Alfred Hölder.

Wieser, F. von (1889) *Der natürliche Werth*. Wien: Alfred Hölder.

Wieser, F. von (1901) "The Austrian School and the Theory of Value." *The Economic Journal*. Vol. 1, March 1891. 108–121.

Wieser, F. von (1914) "Theorie der gesellschaftlichen Wirtschaft." In *Grundriss der Sozialökonomik. Wirtschaft und Wirtschaftwissenschaft*. Bearbeitet von K. Bücher, J. Schumpeter, Fr. Freiherrn von Wieser. Tübingen: Verlag von J.C.B. Mohr (Paul Siebeck). 125–444.

Wieser, F. von (1919) *Recht und Macht. Sechs Vorträge*. Leipzig: Verlag von Duncker & Humblot.

Wieser, F. von (1926) "The Austrian School of Economists." In Higgens H. (ed.), *Palgrave's Dictionary of Political Economy*. Vol. I. A–E. London: Macmillan and Co. 814–818.

Wieser, F. von (1927) "Theorie des Geldes." In *Handwörterbuch der Staatswissenschaften*. Herausgegeben von Ludwig Elster, Adolf Weber, Friedrich Wieser. Jena: Verlag von Gustav Fischer. Vierte Auflage. Vierter Band. Finanzen-Gut. 681–717.

Wieser, F. von (1929a) *Gesammelte Abhandlungen*. Mit einer Biographischen Einleitung. Herausgegeben von Friedrich A. von Hayek. Tübingen: Verlag von J.C.B. Mohr (Paul Siebeck).

Wieser, F. von (1929b) "Das Wesen und der Hauptinhalt der theoretischen Nationalökonomik." In *Gesammelte Abhandlungen*. Mit einer Biographischen Einleitung. Herausgegeben von Friedrich A. von Hayek. Tübingen: Verlag von J.C.B. Mohr (Paul Siebeck). 10–34.

Wieser, F. von (1929c) "Die oesterreichische Schule und die Werttheorie." In *Gesammelte Abhandlungen*. Mit einer Biographischen Einleitung. Herausgegeben von Friedrich A. von Hayek. Tübingen: Verlag von J.C.B. Mohr (Paul Siebeck). 35–125.

Wieser, F. von (1929d) "Ueber das Verhältnis der Kosten zum Wert." In *Gesammelte Abhandlungen*. Mit einer Biographischen Einleitung. Herausgegeben von Friedrich A. von Hayek. Tübingen: Verlag von J.C.B. Mohr (Paul Siebeck). 377–404.

4 Böhm-Bawerk and Capital

Eugen Böhm-Bawerk

Böhm-Bawerk

In 1891, Eugen Böhm-Bawerk responded to a request from the editors of the journal *Annals of the American Academy of Political and Social Science* to write an account of the Austrian School of Economics. Entitled "The Austrian Economists," it appeared in the first volume of that journal. Its German version provides a brief yet comprehensive account of the Austrian School in its first 20 years from the perspective of one of the three founders of this School. While it was written a decade after Böhm-Bawerk's earlier publication, it offers a good starting point because it locates his own relationship to Menger and von Wieser.

Eugen Böhm-Bawerk acknowledges that he is one of the members of the Austrian School and he admits that this might not make him an impartial reporter. However, the survey that he does provide is a rather carefully worded one. He begins by indicating the Austrians' difference with the German Historical School by emphasizing that the primary concern of the Austrians is their focus on theory in the strictest sense of the word. Although he distances the Austrians from the Germans because of their lack of respect for theory, he acknowledges that both schools agree that classical national economy was incomplete. Where they disagreed revolved around what was lacking in the classical writings. For the Germans, it was the wrong method. They felt that the overwhelmingly abstract-deductive method should have been replaced by a mostly inductive approach. In contrast, the Austrians had insisted that the necessary reform of the discipline demanded the replacement of its method. As Böhm-Bawerk indicated, one must leave abstraction and replace it with the "'empirical building blocks'" ("'empirische Bausteine'") of history and statistics (Böhm-Bawerk 1968b: 205–206).

The Germans had regarded the classical approach as being totally wrong; in contrast the Austrians regarded the problems as a typical

DOI: 10.4324/9781003193746-4

"child illness" that should not be replaced but remedied. Böhm-Bawerk insisted that the Austrians were richer for being able to build upon the 100 years of work since the classical national economists wrote but he allowed that the Germans were correct in noting the importance of empirical materials. Their error is in insisting that empiricist information is all that is sufficient—"For without abstraction there is overall no science."[1] Böhm-Bawerk maintains that the most important work was Menger's pioneering *Untersuchungen* but that the Germans failed to grasp that Menger was not disparaging their empiricist interests; he was attempting to show that that interest may be necessary but that it was not sufficient. The German attacks meant that Menger had to have one hand on the plow while the other hand had to hold the sword. It would have been easier for Menger to have been more fruitful if he did not have to be so defensive (Böhm-Bawerk 1968b: 207).

Böhm-Bawerk held that the most important yield of the Austrians was the theory of value. He maintains that the way to determine value is to consider what the need is and what will satisfy it, but the important part is to consider what is missing. He offers as an illustration a farmer who has three sacks of corn. The first one will satisfy his hunger, the second will be held in reserve, while the third will feed his birds. Thus, as the sacks of corn increase, their value to the farmer decreases and this, Böhm-Bawerk says, is its "marginal utility" ("Grenznutzen"). While he insists that this is the main thesis of the Austrian School, he notes that it was Gossen in Germany who had first discovered it. Unfortunately, neither he nor anyone else recognized its importance and it was not until 20 years later, that three different thinkers, from three different countries came to realize its value—the Englishman Jevons, the Swiss Walras, and the Austrian Menger (he suggests that the American Clark came close) (Böhm-Bawerk 1968b: 208–209).

As an illustration, Böhm-Bawerk suggests that a man who has had his winter coat stolen is in need of a replacement so he spends 20 dollars on a new coat. What that means is that he has 20 dollars fewer to spend on other goods. This example shows how the theory hits upon the most important theoretical problem and that is the relationship between inclinations and needs on one side and property and income on the other with price in between both sides. For the Austrians, the answer to this problem is to emphasize that the price is determined by the subjective value. This emphasis differentiates the Austrians from most other economists, but Böhm-Bawerk suggests that there is another difference and that is in connection to the relation between cost and value. Here, he refers to those who contend that cost is the "'ultimate regulator of value'." But the Austrians insist that that is an objective approach that does not answer the question about value and he insists again that it is the person who is in need of something who decides what he is willing to pay—thus value is something that must necessarily be subjective. He explains that this is like the difference between the Ptolomaic and Copernican systems; the Austrians recognize that value is not something "objective" but is a personal and subjective determination (Böhm-Bawerk 1968b: 211–216). After spending a fair number of pages discussing goods (and citing Menger, von Wieser, and himself), Böhm-Bawerk concludes by observing that over the past 40 years, its blind acceptance of its own approach has made it impossible for the German School to advance (Böhm-Bawerk 1968b: 228–229).

The essay on the Austrian School is related to several other essays that Böhm-Bawerk wrote. In "Unsere Aufgaben" from 1892, he departed from the Austrian School's emphasis on theory to note that economics is linked together with social policy and that it is "our tasks" to pursue both theory and practice (Böhm-Bawerk 1968c: 130, 134, 142). And, he notes that economics can help social policy in many cases, and he identifies how important economic thinking was to the development of shipping canals and railways. Economists provided the necessary statistics and the rationale for building the rail lines and linking the rivers (Böhm-Bawerk 1968c: 135).

It is in light of Böhm-Bawerk's concern about both theory and practice that one can read a book review of a lecture than Lujo Brentano had given in Vienna in April of 1888. Brentano's lecture was entitled "Die klassische Nationalökonomie" and Böhm-Bawerk suggests that the title of his review of Brentano's work probably should be amended by prefixing "against" ("Gegen") to it. Brentano objected to the classical national economics because he regarded it an error to reduce human desires to just two: the drive for the greatest advantage and the drive for sex. This oversimplifies things and is indicative of the classical national economists' belief that abstraction can reduce complex human beings to a few basic principles which explain universal human conduct. Böhm-Bawerk notes that this makes people seem like marionettes and that their actions are controlled from above by the use of strings (Böhm-Bawerk 1968d: 144–145). He further contends that, as Lujo Brentano had pointed out, the classical national economists' conviction of the importance of the greatest advantage led them to the belief that value was determined by the amount of labor needed to produce the object. Böhm-Bawerk agrees with Brentano on this point but he objects that Brentano is ready to junk the entire classical project because of this error. Böhm-Bawerk is cognizant of Brentano's mastery, which amounts almost to magic. And, he is tempted to apologize for disturbing Brentano's "artwork" with such a "sober and sobering critique" ("nüchterne und ernüchterende Kritik") (Böhm-Bawerk 1968d: 147).

Böhm-Bawerk indicates that Brentano has three major complaints against the classical national economists. Brentano's first objection was that Adam Smith was so enamored with abstraction that he failed to notice the complexity of the real world. Brentano's second complaint was that Smith's doctrine was completely erroneous and that these errors were then passed down in economics (Böhm-Bawerk 1968d: 147–148). In Brentano's opinion, these errors were in the notions of value, money, and payments for labor. Brentano's third objection is that each and every one of these errors was a result of Adam Smith's infatuation with the idea of abstract individuals. Böhm-Bawerk counters that Brentano's three complaints reveal a real and fundamental understanding of classical national economics and that he intends to provide a corrective to Brentano's appealing but false picture of Adam Smith's approach to economics (Böhm-Bawerk 1968d: 148). He complained that Brentano's conception was similar to that which had been around for decades. It was a superficial reading of the classical national economy, passed down over the past half century in a superficial manner. It was in essence a vulgar account; Böhm-Bawerk signals his intentions to attack it head on.

Brentano placed much of his critical emphasis on the Smith and Ricardo notions of value, and especially, on the role that labor plays in it. Brentano objected to their approach, which he maintained as "exact," "abstract," and even "a priori." For Brentano, the individual is nothing more than an "abstract egoist." However, Böhm-Bawerk suggests that from this faulty premise, Brentano was bound to draw a faulty conclusion. But it was not just Brentano who did this; Schmoller was guilty of a similar mistake (Böhm-Bawerk 1968d: 150–151). Böhm-Bawerk countered that as much as the Historical School seemed to believe in history, it seemed to think that the discipline of national economy should be fully formed as if it had sprung from Zeus' head like Pallas Athena. Yet, national economy has a history that goes back to Adam Smith and its axioms and its theories are the results of years of hard work (Böhm-Bawerk 1968d: 153). To hear Brentano tell it, classical national economics is so misguided that it is like entering Hell and that it should have Dante's inscription over the doorway: "Lasciate ogni Speranza!" (Böhm-Bawerk 1968d: 155). Böhm-Bawerk concludes by making some final observations. The Austrians believe that one can learn from history because it provides a wealth of material. In this sense Brentano is correct. However, Brentano thought that the classical national economists believed in theory without history but that he and his fellow historians were convinced that it should be "history forward, theory back" ("Geschichte voran, Theorie zurück"). But for Böhm-Bawerk, the future requires a third version: "history *and* theory!" ("Geschichte *und* Theorie!") (Böhm-Bawerk 1968d: 156).

In 1896 Böhm-Bawerk published an essay that spelled out in some detail the similarities and the differences between the German Historical School and the Austrian School of Economics. Its title is simply "Historical and Theoretical National Economics" ("Historische und theoretische Nationalökonomie,") and it is another book review—this time it is a review of Gustav Schmoller's 1888 volume *Zur Literaturgeschichte der Staats-und Sozialwissenschaften*. It is not, however, a review of the entire book but only of the portrait of Wilhelm Roscher that Schmoller provides. Böhm-Bawerk begins by both crediting and discrediting the School. He credits the founder and "old master" ("Altmeister") Roscher for his 50 years of service but he disparages Schmoller for stringing together a number of lines that he had written about Roscher over the decades (Böhm-Bawerk 1968g: 157). He does credit Schmoller for detailing how Roscher had begun his academic life as a historian and a philologist and that he gradually turned toward national economics. As a historian, he had a great appreciation of his predecessors and that meant that he had considerable respect for Adam Smith and David Ricardo (Böhm-Bawerk 1968g: 158–159). Böhm-Bawerk notes that Schmoller's book contains many essays on different scholars and different topics so there is no way that he could review each and every essay. However, he does suggest that there is an overarching theme that is connected especially to Roscher and that theme is the issue of the proper method in national economy. And, he admits that the question about the appropriate method is just as pressing as it was several decades ago. He further admits that he is a defender of Menger's so-called exact method but he also declares that he understands the importance of using history and statistics in economics. To emphasize how much regard he has for both the German Historical method and his own theoretical approach, he reminds his readers of his review of Lujo Brentano's published lecture (Böhm-Bawerk 1968g: 161 and note 2). He repeats his claim that Brentano's attack on the "abstract" method was so far-fetched—neither Menger, nor von Wieser, nor himself had ever suggested the type of method that Brentano had attributed to the Austrians. And, Böhm-Bawerk finds it incredulous that someone of the reputation that Brentano has could have ever come up with such an erroneous account

(Böhm-Bawerk 1968g: 162). He suggests that Brentano was ignoring the fact that the deductive method is successfully used in almost every science and it was successfully used in classical national economics. Böhm-Bawerk stresses again that he has nothing against the German Historical School's concern with facts and statistics; in fact, he agrees that much can be learned from analyzing them. What he does have against that School is its dogmatic insistence that facts and statistics are the only things which matter and that its method is the sole method for national economy (Böhm-Bawerk 1968g: 165–168). What makes this even worse is that the Historical School actually engages in deductive reasoning even while denying its worth. Roscher, Knies, and even Hildebrand utilized this method in many of their works— certainly Roscher did in his famous *Grundlagen der Nationalökonomie* and Knies did in his highly regarded *Geld und Kredit*. Böhm-Bawerk even mentions in a footnote that Schmoller admitted that in *Geld und Kredit* that Knies' method was fundamentally identical to that which Menger had used (Böhm-Bawerk 1968g: 174 and note 6). If the older members of the German Historical School used the abstract-deductive method, then how can Schmoller try to discredit it? Böhm-Bawerk answers by indicating that Schmoller and others simply misrepresent the method. They insist that the problem with the abstract-deductive method is that it is totally unempirical and that its hypotheses are too far removed from the real world. It is not just Schmoller who makes such assertions but others like Werner Sombart in his critique of von Wieser's *Natürlichen Werth* (Böhm-Bawerk 1968g: 178–179 and notes 8, 9, and 10). Yet these critics recognize that Menger, von Wieser, Sax, and Böhm-Bawerk are concerned with the real world and real human beings; after all, they often refer to the Austrian School and the "psychological school of national economy" ("'psychologischen Schule der Nationalökonomie'") (Böhm-Bawerk 1968g: 181). Furthermore, the Austrians are not egoists but are concerned with highly important factors such as "economic life, common life, custom, humanity, nationality" ("Wirtschaftsleben, Gewohnheit, Sitte, Humanität, Nationalität") (Böhm-Bawerk 1968g: 181). He suggests that he and his fellow theorists are more than ready to admit their errors—when they make them. But he finds it objectionable for them to be faulted for beliefs that they do not have. And, he also finds troubling that their critics ignore the fact that the German historicists such as Knies, and Wagner used theory in their work on money and credit, and that more recent writers have also used theory in their investigations into value. Böhm-Bawerk concludes his essay with the expressions of hope that the "Methodenstreit" can be safely ended and that both sides can recognize the positives that each side brings to national economics. His greatest hope is that national economy will continue to increase in importance for thinkers around the world and that the combination of undeniable practical results coupled with the abstract-deductive investigations into the truth will win even more converts to their discipline (Böhm-Bawerk 1968g: 186–187).

Shortly before he died, Böhm-Bawerk published a lengthy essay entitled "Power or Economic Law?" ("Macht oder ökonomisches Gesetz?"). The notion of "law" shows the connection of this late essay to his first major publication "Law and the Conditions from the Point of View of the National Economic Doctrine of Goods" ("Recht und Verhältnisse von Standpunkte der volkswirthschaftlichen Güterlehre."). One of the major issues of the later essay focuses on the relationship between social forces and economic analyses and it revolves specifically around the question of the power of these social forces. For Böhm-Bawerk, these forces may be invisible and inchoate or they may be written and formed in the codification of laws. They may be used by capitalists in the form of trusts, cartels, and monopolies or they may be utilized by workers with strikes and boycotts (Böhm-Bawerk 1968f: 233–235). He readily admits that he cannot provide a definitive answer to the question about the relationship between social forces and economic laws but he suggests that he can offer some ideas about the path towards finding such an answer (Böhm-Bawerk 1968f: 240). On the one hand, there is no question that humans have some power over nature but on the other hand it is not so obvious how much a person has economic power over someone else. Nonetheless, Böhm-Bawerk offers two examples where someone has economic power over another. In the first case, it is where a profiteer can exact more money from someone who has borrowed money from him. In the second, those who have a monopoly on a particular good are in a position to determine what price they can charge and expect customers to pay it (Böhm-Bawerk 1968f: 241–243). Yet, he insists that there are human factors which influence these seemingly economic decisions—factors which range from sheer humanity and generosity to racial hatred and vanity. However, it is easy enough to envision a businessman who has such a monopoly that he cannot be bothered by anything other than rational egoism—neither public opinion nor any sense of altruism has any sway over his purely economic decisions—only profit matters to him (Böhm-Bawerk 1968f: 255–256). In such a situation, the workers have no alternative but to respond in such a way that it threatens his profits and that method is the strike (Böhm-Bawerk 1968f: 256–267). But both sides have some power to force the other side to capitulate:

the workers can continue to refuse to work long enough to make the businessman agree to pay higher wages. Yet the businessman may be able to wait long enough for the workers to exhaust their savings. If faced with their families starving or returning to work, many will be forced to choose the latter (Böhm-Bawerk 1968f: 283–284, 289, 292). Böhm-Bawerk insists that he is simply describing situations and is not taking sides. But what he wanted to make clear is that he does not adhere to economic individualism and that he recognizes that capitalists and workers are not just individuals but are also members of groups; thus, economic power cannot be totally divorced from social factors (Böhm-Bawerk 1968f: 297–300). "Macht oder ökonomisches Gesetz?" gives the impression of an old master having to rehash much of what he has said many times before. It has a number of references and in a few he actually cites some of his greatest critics like J.B. Clark. But Böhm-Bawerk also refers numerous times to his own writings. [2] In contrast, *Rechte und Verhältnisse vom Standpunkte der Volkswirtschaftlichen Güterlehre* has a fresh, youthful vitality indicative of this being Böhm-Bawerk's first major work.[3] As a beginning work it also contains a fair number of assertions—assertions that indicate a large sense of certainty, both that he is undoubtedly correct to see what others have failed to see and that there are so many scholars who lack a real understanding. An example of the first is found in the opening sentence where Böhm-Bawerk announces that he has made the attempt to provide "a decisive and an unambiguous solution" ("eine entscheidene und unzweideutige Lösung") to the problem of goods. As an indication of his confidence, he concluded his brief preface with the hope that his work would be met with friendly acceptance (Böhm-Bawerk 1968g: 5–6).

Böhm-Bawerk begins by indicating that there are some issues in political economy that may not seem to be the most pressing but still are questions that demand answers. One of these questions revolves around invisible ideas and how they relate to the doctrine of goods. The two ideas that he has in mind are "*laws* and *conditions*" ("*Rechte und Verhältnisse*"). He does not mean specific laws but legal systems and he does not mean particular conditions but general relations. This is mostly a theoretical issue but he insists that he is also concerned with practical needs (Böhm-Bawerk 1968g: 8). While he insists that political economists are mistaken about debt and credit, there are some who have shed light on this relationship. He gives as an example Henry Dunning Macleod, who he argues is wrong in his *Elements of Political Economy* and Karl Knies as someone who is right in *Der Kredit* (Böhm-Bawerk 1968g: 10 notes 2 and 3). While Böhm-Bawerk restricts his comments on Knies to "very sharp and fundamental," he devotes several pages to criticizing Macleod. He suggests that Macleod's theory rests upon two brief premises: First, if A lends B a Taler, then B possesses a "material good" ("körperliche Gut") with the value of one Taler. Second, in A's demand for the repayment of the loaned Taler, A possesses an "immaterial good" which is not identical to the material good that B possesses (Böhm-Bawerk 1968g: 11). However, to insist that this is a negative good is wrong. Böhm-Bawerk objects that there are no negative goods just as there are no negative things—when someone loans someone an apple, it makes no sense to speak of a negative apple. It is to prevent such economic errors that Böhm-Bawerk insists that he has written this work and that he intends to bring much needed clarity to the discipline—especially in respect to laws and relations can be said to be pertinent to national economics (Böhm-Bawerk 1968g: 13–15).

Böhm-Bawerk notes that he is following Menger's "epoch-making" *Grundsätze* and that means both emphasizing the subjectivity of values and that goods are relevant only to those who recognize that they need them for specific reasons. Thus, like Menger, he is going against almost the entire history of political economics. Böhm-Bawerk explains that there have been three major periods in their discipline: the period before Adam Smith, the period of Adam Smith, and the period of reaction to Adam Smith (Böhm-Bawerk 1968g: 18–20, 23–27). He also points out that for the most part all members of all three periods tended to focus on material goods and the physical possession of them. He suggests that it was only recently that jurists introduced the notion of legal possession as opposed to owning something simply by virtue of force. This is the new category of *"legal possession"* (*"rechtliche Haben"*) in contrast to natural possession (Böhm-Bawerk 1968g: 35). It is the state that guarantees that someone has ownership of something but he allows that ultimately the state's power is ultimately predicated on force (Böhm-Bawerk 1968g: 38–44).

Most of the rest of this work is devoted to the notion of use and it is only towards the end of the essay that Böhm-Bawerk returns to the concept of ownership. He asks whether a person who has purchased something has something more than simply a title of possession. This brings him back to the concept of legal ownership and that this gives the possessor a "legal protection" ("Rechtschutz") (Böhm-Bawerk 1968g: 115–116). This issue becomes especially crucial when it comes to the concept of credit—how can the loaning individual be certain that he will be paid back by the borrower and the answer rests with the legal structure and the power of the state. It also becomes more crucial because capitalism rests on the ability to borrow now with the expectation of future reward. This involves not only money but also time and trust, as well as the *"future existence of goods"* (*"künftige Dasein von Gütern"*) (Böhm-Bawerk 1968g: 124–125). The fact that Böhm-Bawerk emphasized this phrase is indicative of two points about *Rechte und Verhältnisse*. First, Böhm-Bawerk placed numerous passages in emphasis (Böhm-Bawerk 1968g: 7, 39, 47–48, 54, 61, 63, 69, 79, 83–87, 93–95, 98–100, 103, 111, 119–123). Second, it is if Böhm-Bawerk believed that he would be more convincing if he emphasized more and was more acerbic in his criticism. Given that this was his first work, these tendencies might be forgiven. Instead, they became features of his scholarly approach.

The final essay to be discussed in the first half of this chapter is a most intriguing one. First, it is an essay but totals more than 100 pages in length. Second, it is found in a collection of essays whose authors include not only authorities from various countries, it also includes Böhm-Bawerk's major critic John B. Clark.[4] Third, his essay is in the "Festgaben" for Karl Knies; thus further proof that despite its reputed history, the three members of the early Austrian School of Economics had a high degree of respect for many of their German Historical School "opponents." Finally, the subject and the tone of Böhm-Bawerk's essay are notable: the topic is his critique of Marxist theory and the tone is both appreciative and combative. This essay is entitled "Zum Anschluss des Marxschen Systems" and has a brief preliminary remark ("Vorbemerkung") and five major sections, although the final one is more of an appendix.

In the "Vorbemerkung," Böhm-Bawerk maintains that Carl (sic) Marx the writer is a very lucky man because no one would maintain that his books would fall into the categories of being easy to read or easy to understand. His books contain the "ballast" of difficult dialectic and mathematical type deductions—weights that would render other books virtually unreadable. In his acknowledgement of the man that the "Festgaben" honors, Böhm-Bawerk mentioned that Carl (sic) Knies was one of the first economists to take Marx seriously but he found that the Marxist system suffered from serious logical contradictions and methodological defects. Knies had expected that these problems would lessen Marx' influence but the opposite appeared to have happened. In fact, despite the problems in the first volume of *Das Kapital*, his followers continued to believe in his philosophy and expected that any defects in that book would be corrected by the later volumes. Böhm-Bawerk sets out the basic ideas of volume one—that all value is in labor and that the capitalist gains more value because of the worker's labor. However, Böhm-Bawerk observed that there is a contradiction between Marx' theory and facts. Unfortunately, facts and logical proof do not matter to Marx's disciples because they would rather believe in his promises. Even more unfortunate was with the appearance of the second volume of *Kapital* the tension within his system not only did not diminish but actually increased. Böhm-Bawerk has no illusions about the difficulty of convincing Marx' followers that the system suffers from fundamental flaws; however, now that the third and final volume was published in 1894, it was finally time to determine a definite decision regarding the Marxist system. After a 30 year conflict, it was time to determine whether Marx himself has solved the riddle of the tension within his thinking and whether his final system has remained true to the facts or not. This is the task that Böhm-Bawerk suggests he is undertaking in his essay (Böhm-Bawerk 1896: 87–91).

Böhm-Bawerk indicates that the two basic pillars of the Marxist system are the "concept of value" ("Wertbegriff") and "law of value" ("Wertgesetz"). As Marx himself often remarked, without these two, his system would be impossible. But as Böhm-Bawerk notes, Marx' concern is not so much with these two pillars as he is with the value-added notion of labor (Böhm-Bawerk 1896: 96–100, 106–108). Rather than continuing with Böhm-Bawerk's criticism here, we will follow his advice and will address it in the next section on capital (Böhm-Bawerk 1896: 109).

The fifth section is no longer devoted to Marx but is a criticism of Werner Sombart. In 1896, Sombart had not published his great two-volume work *Der moderne Kapitalismus* nor had he joined with Edgar Jaffé and Max Weber to become editors of the *Archiv für Sozialwissenschaft und Sozialpolitk*. While his reputation today is rather minimal, he became one of the most influential political economists. When Weber died in 1920, Sombart was more famous than Weber and his international reputation would continue until the early 1930s. However, in 1896 Sombart was a major follower of Marx. In fact, Böhm-Bawerk suggests that Sombart was Marx' chief apologist and he points to Sombart's recently published essay "Zur Kritik des ökonomischen Systems von Karl Marx" (Böhm-Bawerk 1896: 187).[5]

According to Böhm-Bawerk, Sombart's defense of Marx is rather novel because he suggests that the tension in Marx' system is problematic only if one assumes that the "law of value" ("Wertgesetz") applies to reality. Sombart argued that it is not empirically real but is a "thinking fact" ("gedänkliche Thatsache") and that is has only a "thinking existence" ("gedänkliche Existenz") (see Böhm-Bawerk 1896: 188).

Before investigating the meaning of these comments, he questions whether Marx or any of his adherents would agree with Sombart's defense. Böhm-Bawerk suggests that they would not because they all have insisted that Marx' theory is empirically valid. Rather than pursuing this line of thinking, it is more relevant to return to Sombart's notion of "gedänkliche Thatsache"—it is a "means of help of our thinking" ("Hülfsmittel unseres Denken") (see Böhm-Bawerk 1896: 192, 204). Yet Böhm-Bawerk reminds his readers that Marx' theory of labor is not about an abstraction but is devoted to what Marx refers to as "'embodied labor'" ("'verkörperten Arbeit'") (Böhm-Bawerk 1896: 193, 195). Böhm-Bawerk insists that Marx was a committed realist and believed that values were objective; Sombart's heart might have been in the right place in wanting to defend Marx, but he was wrong in making Marxist theory into a subjective and psychological construct (Böhm-Bawerk 1896: 199–200).[6]

Böhm-Bawerk concludes his critique of the Marxist system by noting that Marx will continue to have a place in the history of social sciences and that is because he has the same combination of traits that his "role model" ("Vorbild") Hegel had. Marx also combined artistic thinking with the fabulous power of erecting countless stages. Like Hegel, Marx also had a wonderous power of mind that ended up constructing something impressive. Unfortunately, it was nothing more than a "house of cards" ("Kartenhaus") (Böhm-Bawerk 1896: 205).[7]

Böhm-Bawerk's writings show a continuation of themes that he developed from Menger and von Wieser about method and value. But they also reveal an aggressive spirit that was mostly missing from his fellow Austrians. Von Wieser rarely indicated that his predecessors made many serious errors and for the most part Menger treated the mistakes that his opponents made more as mistakes made by misguided experts; whereas Böhm-Bawerk hints that his opponents were mostly charlatans or even idiots. In light of this, his treatment of Marx and especially of Sombart is rare: the former seemed unaware of the contradictions in his system and the latter was to be complimented for attempting to defend his master by unconventional means. These are some things that should be kept in mind when focusing on Böhm-Bawerk's key theme—capital and capitalism.

Capital

Böhm-Bawerk's largest, most famous, and most contentious work first appeared in 1884 with the first volume: *Kapital und Kapitalzins*, which carried the subtitle *Geschichte und Kritik der Kapitalzinstheorien*.

As this subtitle indicates, he is not only exploring the history of the theories of capital interest, but also launching a critique of them. Five years later, Böhm-Bawerk published the second volume with the subtitle *Positive Theorie des Kapitales*, which indicated that he was offering his own positive theory of capital. For the third edition, the second volume was published in two "half volumes" ("Erste Halbband" and "Zweite Halbband") and the second "Halbband" contained fourteen appendixes.[8] All three volumes are large: the first volume is almost 750 pages, the first "Halbband" of the second is 650, and even the second "Halbband" is 470. In light of this, only a cursory account of Böhm-Bawerk's most famous book can be given here and it will focus almost exclusively as it relates to capital.[9]

Böhm-Bawerk retains part of the foreword to the first edition, which includes the passages in which he suggests that writing about capital and capital interest does not require any defense. No one would doubt the importance of these topics just as no one would question their massive degrees of difficulty. If anything, the concept of capital is one of the most important concepts in political economy but is also one that had too many competing versions (Böhm-Bawerk 1914: IX). He also justifies dividing his work into two volumes and that the critical historical part needed to be kept separate from the positive theory of capital. But he is defensive regarding the increase in size and insists that he kept the increases in the third edition to less than he had in the second edition. He also seems somewhat defensive about his need to clarify his ideas—a need that will be shown in much more detail in the volume of appendices devoted to answering his critics and clarifying his points.

As Böhm-Bawerk indicates in his subtitle, the first volume is a history and a critique of the previous notions about capital and capital interest. Because it is historical and negative, the examination here will be relatively straightforward and brief. In his opinion, capital and interest are bound together: whoever has capital has a means of income. But unlike labor or investments, capital interest is different. It is different because it flows even if one does not have a "hand" in its development. It also differs because unlike the cessation of labor, it continues to generate (Böhm-Bawerk 1914: 1–3). Unfortunately, the notion of capital interest and even the idea of capital remains contentious; therefore, he provides some definitions and concepts. He admits that the concept of capital is both misused and abused and he offers as a tentative definition a "*complex of produced means of acquisition*" ("*Komplex produzierter Erwerbsmittel*"). He defends this tentative definition first, by noting that it is the one that is most commonly used; and second, by insisting that it is the most useful because it is the most limited. He clarifies that there are two "nuances" which pertain to this general concept of capital. One is the social version and the other is the individual one. He attempts to explain the difference by indicating that a book from a lending library would come under the heading of the individual economy but not under the social one, whereas something produced for consumption either within a country or for export would count as being part of the social economy (Böhm-Bawerk 1914: 7–8). Here he is not so much concerned about capital as he is about the interest that is generated by it and he refers to it as either *"capital rent"* (*"Kapitalrente"*) or *"capital interest"* (*"Kapitalzins"*). He differentiates this interest from the rent or interest from income from rental property or from lending and he maintains that one function of capital interest is the increase in amount—rather than being spent or invested, it simply continues to accrue. He concludes this initial section on "basic concepts" ("Grundbegriffe") by admitting that the whole problem of capital interest is difficult and is resistant to any attempt at mathematical exactness (Böhm-Bawerk 1914: 9–11).

For Böhm-Bawerk, the issue of capital interest grew out of the philosophical and canonical objections to lending because in both usury and in capital interest there is no element of labor and any profit that is gained without work is to be frowned upon or regarded as immoral (Böhm-Bawerk 1914: 12–26). While the moral rejection seemed to fade in antiquity, the Church's fight against lending continued until reaching a highpoint in the fourteenth century. Böhm-Bawerk maintains that it was the Reformer Calvin who first insisted that the canonical prohibition against lending needed to be reconsidered and he maintains that it was the jurist Molinaeus who objected to the doctrine. Böhm-Bawerk tends to keep his examinations focused on facts but there is a hint of admiration as he distinguishes between the two: whereas the legal scholar wrote a lengthy and cautious work filled with distinctions and casuistic, the theologian attacked it with directedness and energy (Böhm-Bawerk 1914: 32–35). Böhm-Bawerk states and criticizes thinkers from France and the Netherlands before turning to Adam Smith and then David Ricardo. More so than Calvin, Smith has Böhm-Bawerk's respect if not admiration. However, he suggests that while Smith was not unaware of the problem of capital interest, he did not appear to investigate it. He did apparently discuss it briefly twice: both in discussing the need to profit from the work of his employees (Böhm-Bawerk 1914: 84 and not 1 and 85 note 2). Böhm-Bawerk observed that at the time Smith wrote, economists tended to strive for neutrality but that his successors were unable to follow that practice. He further observes that they recognized the increasing power of capitalism. He attributes much of this to industrialization, which allowed the capitalist to build factories, employ more workers, increase production with machines, and reap more profits. The question for Smith, and more so for Turgot, was why was there surplus value ("Wertüberschuß" or "Mehrwert")? Böhm-Bawerk is mostly interested in Adam Smith's response which he maintains was the following: "The value surplus must exist because otherwise the capitalist would have no interest in making his capital be used productively." ("Der Mehrwert muß sein, weil der Kapitalist sonst kein Interesse hätte, sein Kapital produktiv zu verwenden.") (Böhm-Bawerk 1914: 92). Böhm-Bawerk suggests that there were five different responses that he lists as the following: 1) the colorless theory; 2) the productive theory; 3) the labor theory; 4) the abstinence theory; and 5) the exploitation theory. Böhm-Bawerk then devotes almost the rest of the entire book to these five theories and their variations.

The Colorless Theory

The first of these theories is the "colorless theory" and he chose the term "colorless" because it a reflection of his belief that the theorists were rather second- and third-rate thinkers. They were found in different countries but they shared a confused and mediocre understanding of economics in general and in the notion about capital interest in particular. Böhm-Bawerk dismisses them with the observation that their thinking is not worth much investigation (Böhm-Bawerk 1914: 95–129).

The Productive Theory

The second theory is the "productivity theory" and he has much more respect for this than he had for the previous one. Unfortunately, the phrase "productivity of capital" has a variety of meanings so Böhm-Bawerk devotes ten pages to discussing these different notions. He suggests that the phrase was instituted by J.B. Say in France but it found acceptance in many parts of Europe. However, it was not evident what he really meant by it. For Böhm-Bawerk, there needs to be clarification regarding two things: first, what does it mean when one states that capital is productive? He answers that it probably means that capital produces goods for later use in contrast to those that are for immediate satisfaction of needs. He differentiates between what he calls "productive goods" ("Produktivgüter") and "consumption goods" ("Genußgüter"). While he appreciates this distinction, he also insists that it is insufficient for a development of a theory of capital interest (Böhm-Bawerk 1914: 131). Second, the adherents of the productive capital insist that it means "more" but they differ on what that "more" means. For some, it means producing "more" goods while for others it means producing "more" value. Regarding the former, Böhm-Bawerk refers to Wilhelm Roscher and illustrates this sense by a fisherman who increases his daily catch from three to thirty fish by utilizing nets. In this sense there are more goods but how does it mean more value? The answer is complex and confusing but he suggests that the increase in value stems from the increase in goods (Böhm-Bawerk 1914: 133–135, 138). However, Böhm-Bawerk agrees that with a boat and nets the fisherman can catch more fish but he does not agree that this adds more value (Böhm-Bawerk 1914: 168–169). In fact, he condemns the productivity thesis for two reasons. First, it fails to deliver what it promised; a failure that was not incidental but a result of the lack of clarity in the term productive. Second, it conflates two things with the claim that by increasing production one increases value. Böhm-Bawerk utilizes an example of a dam that results in more water. That there is more water is indisputable and that water is more in volume but it is not more in value (Böhm-Bawerk 1914: 229–231).

The Labor Theory

The third theory is the "Use" theory ("Nutzungtheorien") and Böhm-Bawerk discusses a number of variations on this theme. But the two that seemed to have attracted his attention the most were the ones by Knies and by Menger. Knies was not an adherent of this theory from the beginning but gradually warmed to it. But when he did, he developed an "uncommonly clear and fundamentally thought-out theory of use" ("Ungemeinenklar und gründlich gedachte Nutzungtheorie") in his two-volume work *Geld und Kredit* (Böhm-Bawek 1914: 260). Although Böhm-Bawerk continued to respect Knies, he took issue with his legal approach to the issue of lending and complained that his understanding about useful goods was misleading. In particular, he suggested that Knies identified "use" ("Nutzung") with "*use* of goods" ("*Gebrauche* von Gütern") (Böhm-Bawerk 1914: 295, 305).

Menger was widely known for developing a "theory of use" ("Nutzungstheorie") but there was a question about value that seemed unresolved: the question regarding the connection between value of an object and the means of its production. Böhm-Bawerk asks whether the value of a thing rests on the means of its production or does the value of the means of production rest on the thing? He suggests that Menger's answer is that the value is always based upon the use of the product and the greater the use, the greater the value (Böhm-Bawerk 1914: 261–262). Unfortunately, Böhm-Bawerk believes that the entire conception of use is convoluted because it takes "use" to be some real existing thing. It is misleading to suggest that there is some "pure use" ("reine Nutzung") (Böhm-Bawerk 1914: 321–322, 327).

The Abstinence Theory

Böhm-Bawerk dispatches the fourth theory quickly. He refers to it as the "abstinence" theory and as with the "colorless" theory proponents, very few reputable scholars were to be found in this group. He reminds the readers that this theory traces its origins back to the labor theory of capital proposed by Adam Smith and was refined by David Ricardo (Böhm-Bawerk 1914: 328–329). While they contended that the source of capital is derived from labor, the proponents of the abstinence theory maintained that capital grew when people did not enjoy the fruits of their labors. Böhm-Bawerk does not so much as criticize this claim as to show that it is too vague. He illustrates this by the example of the person who spends a day planting fruit trees. He is expending the labor now for the rewards in the future; but in his case, they will not be available for ten years. How does this make sense as abstaining from the fruits of one's labor if they will not be there for a decade? (Böhm-Bawerk 1914: 341, 343).

The Exploitation Theory

The fifth theory is given the label "labor" theory yet Böhm-Bawerk contends that this term applies to a group of theories—a main one really about labor and the other primary one about the exploitation of labor. The first one is brief and covers a time frame from Adam Smith to David Ricardo to contemporary French and German theorists. Much of his account is a gloss on his earlier remarks. His criticism is similarly brief and relatively muted although he complains that the German "Katheder-Sozialisten" appear to misuse the idea of work and abuse the notion of capitalism. Böhm-Bawerk's greatest objection to these German professors is their disdain for theory (Böhm-Bawerk 1914: 356–366, 370–376, Böhm-Bawerk 1968e).

Böhm-Bawerk devotes a major portion of this volume to an examination of what he calls the "exploitation theory" ("Ausbeutungstheorie"). This discussion differs from his previous investigations not just in the length (434–565) but because he treats it as a single theory rather than variations on a theme. It also differs because in the case of the former he tended to spend almost equal time on an explanation of the theory and his criticism of it; here, however, he devotes slightly more than 11 pages to the historical overview and close to 120 pages to criticism. Another way of looking at this, is that he mentions more than a dozen figures in the historical overview but spends 44 pages on Marx alone.

The theory of exploitation is a modern theory and one that has drawn enormous attention. Despite this, it does not have a shortened name so Böhm-Bawerk calls it the exploitation theory. He justifies this choice on the grounds that it accurately reflects the theory. That is because all valued goods are produced by human labor but that the worker does not enjoy all of that product. Rather, the worker receives only partial fruits of his labor via his payment by his employer. It is the employer as capitalist who gains more and depending on how hungry (or desperate) the worker is, the employer has more or less leverage over him. As Böhm-Bawerk suggests, the capital interest is a result of that part of the product of a foreign work which comes with the exploitation of the precarious situation of the worker.[10] He considers this a socialist theory; it was Marx who based his own theory on that of Rodbertus. Much of the remainder of this huge section is devoted to a critique of Rodbertus and Marx and stands outside of the focus of this book. However, Böhm-Bawerk notes the connection between "effort" ("Mühe") and "value" ("Wert") and how this connection is found in many of the five theories. But he asks why is the one associated with the other? What about other connections such as the "exchange value" ("Tauschwert")? (Böhm-Bawerk 1914: 447, 513–514, 520). As he had earlier, Böhm-Bawerk is of two minds about Marx' theory. While he acknowledges that there is a certain degree of genius in it, it is full of contradictions and mistakes. But he has no doubt that it has proven to be persuasive for thousands of people and while many have sought to modify and improve it, they all fail in comparison to Karl Marx (Böhm-Bawerk 1914: 543–544, 561–565).

There is a very large appendix to this volume in which Böhm-Bawerk addresses the attempts to explain capital interest since he first published this volume. Hence, the period is from 1884 to 1914. As this appendix is part of his criticism, it is understandable that he does not think that his contemporaries have gotten any closer to understanding capital interest. He does grant that John Bates Clark and Irving Fischer have made major strides but he objects that Clark's notion of "true capital" does not seem to mean anything (Böhm-Bawerk 1914: 623). He is dismissive of the Italians, although he thinks that Pareto is the most intriguing of them. The French, Dutch, and others fare no better. Of the Germans, he does seem to approve of Schumpeter because he is mostly in agreement with Böhm-Bawerk (Böhm-Bawerk 1914: 624–631).

The second part of *Kapital und Kapitalzins* is titled *Positive Theorie des Kapitales* and the third edition carries the forward to the first and third editions. For the first edition, Böhm-Bawerk explains the unexpected delay between the appearance of the first half and the publication of this second half on the difficulty in researching and writing his positive theory. He also places some responsibility on the fact that what he is providing is essentially a whole new theory of capital. He allows that his examination is on both value ("Wert") and capital ("Kapital") and that others have dealt with the former, but he insists that the second is groundbreaking. His main concern is not with its novelty but with its degree of abstractness. Yet, he insists that his examination is rooted in reality and he is devoted to empirical exploration (Böhm-Bawerk 1909: XVIII–XIX). In the Forward to the third edition, he explained that his obligations made it impossible to revise the second edition and it has been only after he had been released from his government responsibilities that he was able to return to his work. He readily acknowledges that many books and articles have appeared during the intervening 20 years and that he has welcomed the growing theoretical interest in the notion of capital. He also offers three points: first, that he has tried to keep to the thread of his argument and has steered clear of engaging with his critics; second, that far from ignoring them, he has taken their comments into consideration, but has been more self-critical; and third, he offers a semi-apology for the lack of stylistic beauty because he deemed it more important to express his thoughts clearly rather than express them in a pleasing style (Böhm-Bawerk 1909: VII–VIII, XVI).

In the brief three-page Introduction ("Einleitung") Böhm-Bawerk observes that the name and theory of capital is found in two areas of economics: the first time in the "doctrine of production" ("Lehre von Produktion") and the second time in the "doctrine of the distribution of goods" ("Lehre von der Verteilung der Güter"). In the first case, capital is regarded as a factor or a tool of production and is considered a means of increasing goods. In the second case, it is considered as a source of income. That is why he divides his book into two parts: the first on capital as a tool and the second on capital as a form of interest. He clarifies this by pointing out that someone who owns an apartment building or someone who owns a special lending library gets "capital" by virtue of being paid; yet, one cannot suggest that those individuals are producing things (Böhm-Bawerk 1909: 1–3).

The *Positive Theorie des Kapitals* is composed of four "books": the first two are on capital as a form of production and the second two are on capital as a means of interest. The focus here is on the first two "books": "Buch" I on "Concept and Essence of Capital" ("Begriff und Wesen des Kapitales") and "Buch" II on "Capital as Tool of Production" ("Das Kapital als Produktionswerkzeug"). "Buch" I has four chapters of differing lengths: the first, second, and fourth are each under 20 pages while the third chapter is 100. In contrast, "Buch" II also has four chapters but they are all almost equal in length. As is evident by the titles of the two "books," the most important one is the first book on the concept and essence of capital.

Böhm-Bawerk takes issue with the idea that there are natural goods—while there are things like berries to pick and eat, these are not very many. In contrast, humans need to do quite a bit in order to make use of something. For example, salt needs to be found, refined, and distributed in order to be useful. In a similar way, Böhm-Bawerk takes exception to the notion that humans create things. It is not as if they are able to create something out of nothing; rather, they work on the thing to make it useable (Böhm-Bawerk 1909: 10–14).

The end goal of all production is the producing of things that will satisfy our needs and these are "goods of the first order" ("Gütern erster Ordnung"). These are produced by combining our own natural power with the natural powers of the external world; in other words, we work on matter to produce things that we need and use. Böhm-Bawerk maintains that there are degrees of difference among the things that we need and he illustrates this by the following example. A man needs and desires water to drink and there is a spring some distance from his house. He can satisfy his thirst by several means: every time he is thirsty, he can go to the spring and drink with his hands. This is the most direct way and it satisfies his thirst immediately. But it is also the most uncomfortable because he must do this every time he gets thirsty. It is also the most insufficient because he cannot collect any more water that what he needs right then. There is another means: here the man constructs a pail out of wood and treks to the spring once daily in order to collect enough water to last him all day. Of course, he had to find a tree and find an axe to cut it down with before he could fashion his pail. There is a third means: instead of cutting down one tree to make one pail, he could cut down many and make a wooden pipeline from the spring to his house. In contrast to the second and even more to the first, this way is the most work intensive. Yet after it is finished, it is the least work intensive because it brings fresh water to his house continuously (Böhm-Bawerk 1909: 16–17). From this and two other examples, Böhm-Bawerk says that the lesson is clear: the longer, indirect means produces more results than the shorter, direct means; this, he claims, is the most important principle of the entire theory of production. This longer and smarter way is nothing less than the notion of capitalistic production and he emphasizes this definition: *"Capital is nothing other than the entirety of the intermediate products."*[11]

The third chapter is a book-length discussion of the conflict over the concept of capital ("Streit um den Kapitalsbegriff"). As both the title and the concluding remarks indicate, this large section is focused on the differences of opinion regarding the notion of capital. It is comprised of four sections: a history of the term until the end of the nineteenth century; his positive suggestion; several other contenders; and a conclusion. Böhm-Bawerk did not always provide a linear account, and this chapter is one of the most difficult ones to follow. Accordingly, rather than trying to discuss each section individually, there will be considerable overlap.

The term capital was originally used to refer to money lending; hence, for Böhm-Bawerk there is a close and natural connection between capital and capital interest (Böhm-Bawerk 1909: 23–29). While he credits Turgot with altering the meaning, he suggests that it was Adam Smith who distinguished between goods used immediately and goods kept for much later use. He was also the one who formulated the notion of the "means of production" and introduced the idea of private economy (Böhm-Bawerk 1909: 31–38). Böhm-Bawerk briefly mentions J.B. Clark and Irving Fisher's contributions and the latter is singled out for his recognition of the importance of time in the conception of capital. Marshall is also complimented for his distinction between "trade-capital" and "social-capital"; unfortunately, none of these three scholars had offered a concise definition of capital (Böhm-Bawerk 1909: 45–52). Instead, in the second section, he offers as a suggestion the following definition: *"In general, we name capital a totality of products which serve as the means of the production of goods."* *("Kapital überhaupt nennen wir einen Inbegriff von Produkten, die als Mittel des Gütererwerbes dienen.")* (Böhm-Bawerk 1909: 54). The third section is the longest and it is devoted to criticizing some of his rivals' suggestions. The two that he concentrates on are Knies and Menger. He believed that there was not much need to attack Roscher because Knies had done a thorough job. He cites Knies' definition from *Geld:* capital is the saving of something for the satisfaction of a need in the future (Böhm-Bawerk 1909: 61 note 1, 63; Knies 1873: 83 and 92). Böhm-Bawerk approves of Knies' definition except for the "little words" ("Wörtchen") *"in the future" (in der Zukunft")* and he complains that Knies never explained what that really meant (Böhm-Bawerk 1909: 63–65).

Carl Menger figures even more prominently in this chapter and both in the first and the third sections. In the first section, he offers considerable praise for Menger's remarkable historical and critical investigations into the fundamentals of economics. He also praised him for those investigations having led him to reject the contemporary definition of capital and insisting on returning to a real concept of capital (Böhm-Bawerk 1909: 46–47). In the third section, he complimented Menger's impressive logical abilities, but he takes issue with Menger's notion of a "natural factor" ("Naturfaktor") meaning natural things. Menger was addressing Adam Smith's notion of working on a piece of property and how labor on it produces capital (Menger 1970a: 150–151). But Böhm-Bawerk apparently objects to Menger's ignoring his own distinction between different orders of goods (Böhm-Bawerk 1909: 88–89 note 1). He also seems to criticize Menger's use of capital to refer to income because this is often the popular notion of capital but is clearly wrong (Böhm-Bawerk 1909: 93–95 and note 1; Menger 1970a: 5, 174). As much as Böhm-Bawerk respected both Menger and Knies, he was not reluctant to criticize them when he thought they had erred.

The fourth and concluding section is short; in it, he apologizes for having had to write such a lengthy and critical section; however, he stressed that it was necessary because the conflict over what capital means has endured for centuries. He was hopeful, however, that his positive suggestion will be accepted (Böhm-Bawerk 1909: 113–114, 121–122).

The fourth and final chapter is a brief and tangential discussion of the differences between what is called "social capital" and "private capital." The former encompasses the means of production while the latter relates to the produced goods. (Böhm-Bawerk 1909: 125–127). In other words, it is the contrast between the socialist proponents like Marx and the scholars of capitalism such as Adam Smith. As the next "Buch" will show, Böhm-Bawerk's understanding of the function of capitalism will reveal an appreciation for the theory of labor but a greater understanding about capital and production.

The second "Buch" on capital and production has two sections, which are not very relevant to this account of capital. First, because Böhm-Bawerk allows that he had already discussed the capital process in the second chapter of the previous "Buch." Second, because he offers a very simplified account by insisting that there are two and only two factors of "productive powers" ("Produktivkräften"): nature and labor and the product is formed by a combination of the two. He repeats what he had said earlier regarding the claim that the longer means of production produces the best product; however, he now admits that this method is a "waste of time" ("Opfer an Zeit") (Böhm-Bawerk 1909: 143 note 2, 145–149). He concludes this section by emphasizing his final observation: that the capitalistic method of production sacrifices time in order to produce a greater number or mass of products—the more time invested yields a greater capital product (Böhm-Bawerk 1909: 160–161). After discussing some associated aspects of production in the second section, Böhm-Bawerk turns to the issue of the function of capital in production. He suggests that there have been two approaches to the role of capital in production: as a "symptom" but not a "cause" and as a "cause" and not a "symptom." He rejects the first as being rather meaningless and concentrates on the second. He reminds us that products are made by the combination of natural things and human labor and he adds that many national economists prefer to regard capital as a form of natural power. He objects that that is not natural because it is directly tied to people; thus, other national economists speak of capital as a "tool of production" ("Produktionswerkzeug"). It differs from the other two in that capital can offer a new means of production compared to the usual combination of nature and labor. In addition, it can add more to the future than the typical combination. At least, these are the reasons that many national economists offer for thinking of capital as the third factor of production (Böhm-Bawerk 1909: 173–175).

Böhm-Bawerk takes issue with this claim that capital is a third factor. He offers an illustration of a man who throws a stone that hits another man and kills him. He asks: did the stone kill the man? The answer is that the stone was the means by which the man was killed, but that it was the man who threw the stone who killed the other person. Böhm-Bawerk insists that capital is like that stone and that capital is not a separate function but is a byproduct ("Zwischenprodukt") of nature and labor—"nothing more" ("weiter nichts") (Böhm-Bawerk 1909: 175–177).

The fourth section is the important one on the theory of capital acquisition ("Die Theorie der Kapitalbildung") and Böhm-Bawerk indicates that currently there are three opinions circulating about this matter. The first one is that capital increases by saving; the second is that it increases because of labor; while the third is that it increases as a result of the combination of both. He indicates that the third view is the widest held and that it is also the correct one. He believes it easy to dismiss the first theory by insisting that Robinson Crusoe cannot improve his lot merely by saving (Böhm-Bawerk 1909: 181–185). The second one is not so easy to reject, but not many industries gain in capital solely by work and that there are other factors which enter into production besides labor (Böhm-Bawerk 1909: 197). This leaves the third one; he illustrates this theory by way of a person who makes a hammer. He needs to use it in order to produce more but he cannot use it indiscriminately or carelessly or else it will be misused or worn out (Böhm-Bawerk 1909: 201,

207, 209). It is here that he breaks off his discussion of capital and takes up the concept of capital interest, and ends the discussion of capital in the positive theory of capital.

The second "Halbband" of the *Positive Theorie des Kapitales* contains fourteen appendices and they are primarily explanations, clarifications, and rebuttals of criticisms. In light of this, it is not necessary to spend too much time in covering this. In addition, some of the appendices are either very brief ("Exkurs XIV" is not even three pages in length) or limited to a very specific issue ("Exkurs IV is on selection). However, Böhm-Bawerk makes a number of important comments in these appendices and some of them provide a window on his thinking and his response to criticism. Regarding the latter, Böhm-Bawerk seems to vacillate between being incredulous about the ability of his critics to misrepresent, misinterpret, and misread what he has written and being someone thankful that some of these thinkers can actually admit that they agree with some of his points. In one footnote, he writes that he "cannot expressly emphasize enough" that he is talking about a technical issue and not making a general observation and in another passage, he is addressing the past, present, and immediate future capitalistic production and is not forecasting into the distant future. In another footnote, he complains that he is being unfairly accused of promoting an "absolute absurdity" and later he objects to the imputation of the universality of natural laws when his economic rules are simply generalities (Böhm-Bawerk 1912: 20 note 1, 28, 30, 99).

Böhm-Bawerk has real objections to some of the criticism. One in particular revolves around the issue of the shortening of the period of production. He offers several instances where time has been saved: previous generations needed to build ships and outfit them in order to sail and then go into the Arctic ocean to hunt whales for whale oil. Now there are places nearby where one can simply drill for oil (Böhm-Bawerk 1912: 66–68, 73). In another place he argues that there can be little doubt that modern tools help shorten the time needed to produce things—certainly modern machines increase production numbers and do so in less time than anyone producing the goods by hand (Böhm-Bawerk 1912: 88–89). Finally, he addresses the question of regularity and objectivity by discussing rail lines. There are many ways to travel by train from Hamburg to Frankfurt am Main, but there is only one that is actually shorter than all the rest. This can be measured either by time or by distance and everyone can agree that it is indeed the shortest. One can also determine the shortest route from Hamburg to Munich—there will be more possibilities but there can be little question which is the shortest distance or the shortest time as this is a "pure objective fact" ("rein objektive Tatsache") (Böhm-Bawerk 1912: 113). However, the choice between two different methods of production cannot be so accurately and minutely calculated. Therefore, it is more a question of choice (Böhm-Bawerk 1912: 124–125).

The "Exkurs" that has the most relevance for this study is the lengthy one entitled "Regarding the Theory of Value of Complimentary Goods" ("betreffend die Theorie des Wertes der komplimentären Güter") because it both deals with the "theory of calculation" ("Theorie der Zurechnung") and because it is a defense of Böhm-Bawerk's theory against von Wieser. In addition, he invokes Menger for having a similar approach to calculation as his own. He notes that the theory of value of complimentary goods is a minor logical branch of economics but one that is necessary and is crucial to any genuine theory of distribution. It is also one that has attracted increasing attention over the past 20 years (Böhm-Bawerk 1912: 173). He divides the economists who have been examining this issue into four groups: The most numerous is the American group led by J.B. Clark. These thinkers contend that the problem is certainly solvable. The second group, which is also numerous, is just as firmly convinced that the issue cannot be solved. In a footnote, he lists Gustav Schönberg. The third group is rather small and merely skeptical about answering the question. In another footnote, he lists Gustav Cassel and Robert Liefmann. Finally, there is a smaller group whose members have devoted considerable effort to the issue of calculation; here, Böhm-Bawerk identifies von Wieser but adds that Schumpeter has also recently addressed it (Böhm-Bawerk 1912: 174 and notes 1, 2, and 3). Böhm-Bawerk allowed that he had no need to say anything to those who doubted the solvability of the problem of calculation because von Wieser had said it better than he possibly could and he draws attention to von Wieser's claim in *natürliche Werthe* that the problem not only can be solved but must be solved (Böhm-Bawerk 1912: 175, von Wieser 1889: 73, 76). Böhm-Bawerk admits that in many points, he is in agreement with von Wieser, but he insists that von Wieser misunderstands him and Menger when he imputes an error in calculating supply and demand and that Böhm-Bawerk and Menger have a genuine understanding about the use of an object (Böhm-Bawerk 1912: 195–197). Böhm-Bawerk applauds von Wieser for differentiating the issue of calculation from that of legal distribution but he complains that he did not differentiate clearly enough between the legal obligations about calculation-distribution and economic considerations (Böhm-Bawerk 1912: 200). Böhm-Bawerk suggests that he and von Wieser do not totally disagree; rather, it is merely a difference of an opinion regarding an important but small issue.

There are two groups of opponents for Böhm-Bawerk: those he really dislikes and those he actually admires. He had evident disdain for the Swedish economist Gustav Cassel and apparently even more for the French thinker Adolphe Landry. While Böhm-Bawerk seemed to think somewhat highly of Cassel's positive works, he thought that Cassel misunderstood his writing. Regarding Landry, Böhm-Bawerk apparently thought that either he had no real understanding of economic theory or that he was especially obtuse when he came to his theories. In contrast, Böhm-Bawerk often offers considerable praise for his critics. He refers approvingly to the American John Bates Clark and his book on the distribution of wealth as having certain points of brilliance. He also had a certain degree of admiration for the noted American Irving Fisher. There is no question of the respect that he held for his fellow Austrians Menger and von Wieser. He also applauds the Austrian Joseph Schumpeter for his insightfulness; however, he complains about his radicalism (Böhm-Bawerk 1912 98 note 1). In light of this, Böhm-Bawerk's reputation for polemics is slightly exaggerated.

Perhaps the best evaluation of Böhm-Bawerk's personal and professional reputation is found in Carl Menger's piece, which was written shortly after Böhm-Bawerk's death. Menger wrote that he was a real privy councilor, a member of the upper house of parliament, and the recipient of numerous high orders. He had been president of the Royal Academy of Sciences (Kaiserlichen Akademie der Wissenschaften) in Vienna and was awarded an honorary doctorate from the university in Heidelberg (Menger 1970c: 294). Perhaps the best evaluation of Böhm-Bawerk's scholarship came from von Wieser. In his *Palgrave* entry he wrote: "Böhm-Bawerk's theory of interest has found staunch adherents and obstinate opponents in equal numbers. But even if one disagrees with its root ideas, it is impossible not to recognize the profound insight which Böhm-Bawerk acquired in his researches in economic theory." (von Wieser 1926: 826). As Menger noted, although he had numerous opponents, he certainly did not have a single enemy (Menger 1970c: 295).

Concluding Comments

Eugen Böhm-Bawerk may not have had Menger's originality, nor von Wieser's ability to explain, but he did have tenacity and the willingness to attack his critics. Von Wieser tended to be polite and accommodating so he did not have very many academic enemies. Menger was misunderstood by some of the members of the German Historical School and was singled out for criticism, but most of his critics' complaints were about his method. In contrast, Böhm-Bawerk seemed to relish intellectual battles and he appeared to welcome the challenges from scholars in Europe and in North America. Yet, even his most ardent critics admired his dedication to his discipline and his willingness to defend his theories at almost any cost.

The early Austrians were frequently accused of being pure theorists, yet their lives serve to refute that characterization. Although Menger never formally served in the Austrian government, his early career in journalism and his concern about economic issues should dispel the notion that he was simply an ivory tower theorist. In addition, he did serve as companion and teacher to Crown Prince Rudolf. In contrast, both von Wieser and Böhm-Bawerk served with considerable distinction in the Austrian government; the latter was especially regarded as having made fundamental contributions to finance. Menger specifically points out that during each of the three periods in which Böhm-Bawerk was involved in the government's financial office, he made lasting contributions. In particular, Menger praised him for reforming the tax system and noted that his service as finance minister would by itself be sufficient to guarantee a place of honor in the history of Austria (Menger 1970c: 295). While those who know something about the "Methodenstreit" may be familiar with the name Carl Menger, it was Böhm-Bawerk whose fame spread farther than either that of Menger or von Wieser.

Notes

1 "Denn ohne Abstraktion gibt es überhaupt keine Wissenschaft." Böhm-Bawerk 1968b: 206.

2 Böhm-Bawerk 1968a: 232 note 2, 233 note 3, 234 note 4, 237 notes 7 and 8, 239 notes 9 and 10, 239 notes 11 and 12, 242 note 14, 246 notes 16–18, 251 note 20, 262 notes 21 and 22, 263 notes 23 and 24, 264 note 25, 265 note 26, 269 note 27, 274 note 28, 276 note 29, 282 note 32.

3 It was his "Habilitationschrift" and was published in 1881. It was the work that earned him the appointment to his first professorship.

4 John Clark's short essay is "The Unit of Wealth" and like Böhm-Bawerk's essay is rather theoretical. Several of the others are devoted to specific issues: Eberhard Gothein focused on agrarian-political changes in the Rhineland and Otto von Boenigk devoted his rather brief contribution to the anti-Chinese movement in America.

5 Earlier Böhm-Bawerk had praised Sombart's essay as being a clear and comprehensive account of Marx' third volume of *Das Kapital* and noted that it was a full and spirited essay. Böhm-Bawerk 1896: 108 note 1. He also notes that he believes that what Marx wrote in the third volume contradicts what he wrote in the first and that even someone as sympathetic to Marx' theory as Sombart has to shake his head in amazement ("'ein allgemeines Schütteln des Kopfes'"). See Böhm-Bawerk 1896: 111.

6 Böhm-Bawerk refrains from suggesting that Sombart, who was a student of Schmoller and a member of the German Historical school, is moving

into Austrian thinking with the subjective defense of Marx. Sombart's notion that the "concept of value" ("Wertbegriff") is a conceptual tool and a heuristic device precedes Max Weber's notion of the "ideal type". There are several instances in which Sombart's thinking seems to have influenced Weber's, but today few scholars are willing to regard Sombart's work as worthy of examination. As one indication of the lack of interest in Sombart, Blaug's collection of essays does not even mention him. Blaug 1992. One hopes that in the near future that might change and that Sombart might regain some of the respect that he had during much of his lifetime.

7 Böhm-Bawerk's critique was answered in 1904 by Rudolf Hilferding, who was just as argumentative as Böhm-Bawerk was but less appreciative. He accuses Böhm-Bawerk of missing, if not distorting, Marx's thinking and repeatedly refers to Böhm-Bawerk's essay as nothing more than a polemic. Hilferding 1973: 162, 166, 168. He also rejects the subjectivism of the early Austrian School and insists that its emphasis on the individual eliminates political economy. Hilferding 1973: 182–183, 190–191. His essay is also almost as long as Böhm-Bawerk's. This exchange is worth its own investigation and it has been the topic of a 1926 dissertation. Unfortunately, I have been unable to locate a copy of Bernhard Rüther's *Die Auseinandersetzung zwischen Eugen von Böhm-Bawerk und Rudolf Hilferding über Karl Marx.*

8 The edition that is used here is the third edition because it was the last one issued during Böhm-Bawerk's lifetime and represents his final views. The edition is somewhat odd because the first "Halbband" of second volume was published in 1909 and the second "Halbband" in 1912. The first volume appeared in 1914 just before Böhm-Bawerk's death. What makes this even more confusing is while the cover and the title page to the *Positive Theorie des Kapitales* has the year 1909, the "Forward to the Second Half-Volume" ("Vorwart zum zweiten Halbband") is dated June 1912. Böhm-Bawerk 1909: II, III, and VI.

9 Böhm-Bawerk's book carries the title *Capital and Capital Interest* but his work on the latter problem will mostly be ignored here. That is in part because of limitations of space but it is more so because it is far more debatable than his work on capital. Menger was reported to have told Schumpeter that the "time will come when people will realize that Böhm-Bawerk's theory is one of the greatest errors ever committed." But others have pointed out that he did not quite agree with his definition of capital, with the implication that he was in disagreement about interest. See Endres 1992: 210 note 2. In addition, in his 1888 article "Zur Theorie des Kapitals" Menger quotes or refers to Böhm-Bawerk many times. Of course, one can argue that Menger may have grown less impressed with Böhm-Bawerk over time but his "Böhm-Bawerk" argues against that. Menger 1970b: 140 note 1, 143 note 2, 147 note 2, 163 note 1, 169 note 1, 182–183 note 2.

10 This is an approximation of what he writes and it does not reflect the emphasis that is in the original: *"Der Kapitalzins besteht also in einem Teile des Produktes fremder Arbeit, erworben durch die Ausbeutung der Zwangslage der Arbeiter."* Böhm-Bawerk 1914: 435.

11 *"Das Kapital aber ist nichts anderes als der Inbegriff der Zwischenprodukte, die auf den einzelnen Etappen des ausholenden Umweges zur Entstehungs kommnen."* Böhm-Bawerk 1909: 18–19, 21.

References

Blaug, M., (ed.) (1992) *Eugen von Böhm-Bawerk (1851–1914) and Friedrich von Wieser(1851–1926)*. Aldershot: Edward Elgar Publishing.

Böhm-Bawerk, E. (1896) "Zum Abschluss des Marxschen Systems." In *Festgaben für Karl Knies*. Herausgegeben von Otto Freiherrn von Boenigk. Berlin: Verlag von O. Haering. 85–205.

Böhm-Bawerk, E. (1909) *Kapital und Kapitalzins. Zweite Abteilung: Positive Theorie des Kapitales*. Innsbruck: Verlag der Wagner'schen Universitäts-Buchhandlung. Dritte Auflage. Erster Halbband. (Buch 1 und 2).

Böhm-Bawerk, E. (1912) *Kapital und Kapitalzins. Zweite Abteilung: Positive Theorie des Kapitales*. Innsbruck: Verlag der Wagner'schen Universitäts-Buchhandlung. Dritte Auflage. Zweiter Halbband. (Buch 3 und 4).

Böhm-Bawerk, E. (1914) *Kapital und Kapitalzins. Erste Abteilung. Geschichte und Kritik der Kapitalzinstheorien*. Innsbruck: Verlag der Wagner'schen Universitäts-Buchhandlung. Dritte Auflage.

Böhm-Bawerk, E. (1968a) *Gesammelte Schriften von Eugen von Böhm-Bawerk*. Herausgegeben von Franz X. Weiss. Frankfurt a. M.: Verlag Sauer & Auvermann. Unveränderter Nachdruck der Ausgabe 1924.

Böhm-Bawerk, E. (1968b) "Die österreichische Schule." In *Gesammelte Schriften von Eugen von Böhm-Bawerk*. Herausgegeben von Franz X. Weiss. Frankfurt a. M.: Verlag Sauer & Auvermann. Unveränderter Nachdruck der Ausgabe 1924, 1968 b, c, d, e. 205–229.

Böhm-Bawerk, E. (1968c) "Unsere Aufgaben." In *Gesammelte Schriften von Eugen von Böhm-Bawerk*. Herausgegeben von Franz X. Weiss. Frankfurt a. M.: Verlag Sauer & Auvermann. Unveränderter Nachdruck der Ausgabe 1924. 129–143.

Böhm-Bawerk, E. (1968d) "Die klassische Nationalökonomie." In *Gesammelte Schriften von Eugen von Böhm-Bawerk*. Herausgegeben von Franz X. Weiss. Frankfurt a. M.: Verlag Sauer & Auvermann. Unveränderter Nachdruck der Ausgabe 1924. 144–156.

Böhm-Bawerk, E. (1968e) "Historische und theoretische Nationalökonomie." In *Gesammelte Schriften von Eugen von Böhm-Bawerk*. Herausgegeben von Franz X. Weiss. Frankfurt a. M.: Verlag Sauer & Auvermann. Unveränderter Nachdruck der Ausgabe 1924. 157–187.

Böhm-Bawerk, E. (1968f) "Macht oder ökonomisches Gesetz." In *Gesammelte Schriften von Eugen von Böhm-Bawerk*. Herausgegeben von Franz X. Weiss. Frankfurt a. M.: Verlag Sauer & Auvermann. Unveränderter Nachdruck der Ausgabe 1924. 230–300.

Böhm-Bawerk, E. (1968g) "Rechte und Verhältnisse. von Standpunkte der Volkswirtschaftlichen Güterlehre. Kritische Studie." In *Gesammelte Schriften von Eugen von Böhm-Bawerk*. Herausgegeben von Franz X. Weiss. Frankfurt a. M.: Verlag Sauer & Auvermann. Unveränderter Nachdruck der Ausgabe 1924. 3–126.

Endres, A.M. (1992) "The Origins of Böhm-Bawerk's 'Greatest Error': Theoretical Points of Separation from Menger." In *Eugen von Böhm-Bawerk (1851–1914) and Friedrich von Wieser(1851–1926)*. In Blaug. 1992. 210–228.

Hilferding, R. (1973) "Böhm-Bawerks Marx-Kritik." In *Aspekte der Marxschen Theorie 1. Zur methodischen Bedeutung des 3. Bandes des "Kapital."* Herausgegeben von Friedrich Eberle. Frankfurt am Main: Suhrkamp. 1973. 130–192.

Knies, K. (1873) *Geld und Kredit. Das Geld. Darlegung der Grundlehren von dem Gelde, mit einer Vorerörterung über das Kapital und die Uebertragung der Nutzungen.* Berlin: Weidmannsche Buchhandlung.

Menger, C. (1970a) "Gesammelte Schriften." In *Kleinere Schriften zur Method und Geschichte der Volkswirtschaftslehre.* Herausgegben mit einer Einleitung und einem Schriftenverzeichnis von F.A. Hayek. Band III.. Tübingen: Verlag von J.C.B. Mohr (Paul Siebeck).

Menger, C. (1970b) "Zur Theorie des Kapitals." In *Kleinere Schriften zur Method und Geschichte der Volkswirtschaftslehre.* Herausgegben mit einer Einleitung und einem Schriftenverzeichnis von F.A. Hayek. Band III. Tübingen: Verlag von J.C.B. Mohr (Paul Siebeck). 133–183.

Menger, C. (1970c) "Eugen v. Böhm-Bawerk." In *Kleinere Schriften zur Method und Geschichte der Volkswirtschaftslehre.* Herausgegben mit einer Einleitung und einem Schriftenverzeichnis von F.A. Hayek. Band III. Tübingen: Verlag von J.C.B. Mohr (Paul Siebeck). 293–307.

Wieser, F. von (1926) "Böhm-Bawek, Eugen von." In *Palgrave's Dictionary of Political Economy.* Edited by Henry Higgs. London: Macmillan and Co. Vol. I. A–E. 825–826.

5 Conclusion

The previous four chapters were conceived as a means to provide an independent and objective account of the thinking of Carl Menger, Friedrich von Wieser, and Eugen Böhm-Bawerk. They were intended to provide a general conception of the thinking of the three figures, as well as a close reading of the three key notions of money, value, and capital. How close I came to achieving that goal may be best determined by the reader. This chapter is an intentional departure from that cool detachment; it is instead, judgmental. It is judgmental in the sense that 1) I attempt to distill what I think is important in the previous main chapters; 2) I evaluate the criticisms that were leveled at the three Austrians during their lifetimes and then some of those lodged against them by later critics; 3) I offer a brief assessment of Max Weber's relation to Menger, von Wieser, and Böhm-Bawerk by addressing Weber's connection to the German Historical School and the Early Austrian School; 4) finally, I offer a justification of why I think scholars should read these three thinkers and why I believe the Early Austrian School of Economics has relevance for today's social-economic scholars. If I have erred on the side of "cool distance" in the main portion of this book, I may have erred on the side of "hot passion" in this final chapter. But as Max Weber insisted in *Wissenschaft als Beruf,* both are necessary for scholarship (Weber 1994: 83–84). It is my contention that too many scholars have overlooked the important theoretical innovations developed by Menger, von Wieser, and Böhm-Bawerk and have either underestimated their contributions or misunderstood their economic principles. After writing this book, my conviction has grown that the writings by these members of the Early Austrian School of Economics deserve serious investigation.

DOI: 10.4324/9781003193746-5

Summary

In this section, I provide the summary of the three main chapters. In Chapter 2, the focus was on the writings of Carl Menger. While commentators have largely dealt with his methodological writings, I have focused more on those devoted to the concept of money. Chapter 3 outlined the work of Friedrich von Wieser. In this case, the central theme of value is shared with other commentators, though I have sought to locate it within his overall thinking about value in social economics. Commentators have sometimes looked at Eugen Böhm-Bawerk's conception of value and have sought to contrast it with von Wieser's. The central focus of Chapter 4 was instead on his concept of capital. Here, value, money, and interest have joined together, but the primary focus remained his definition of capital and how it functions. In each of these chapters I have sought to provide a general account of their writings as well as a focus on what I took to be the central theme of their work. With each of these thinkers I have tried to show that the sum of their work is greater than their parts.

Criticism

In this section, I provide a summary of sorts of four different complaints about the Early Austrian School. In most of the German accounts of the "Methodenstreit," the Austrians are accused of being anti-German. But as I showed in Chapter 2, Menger first sought approval by the members of the German Historical School and as Chapters 2, 3, and 4 indicated, Menger, von Wieser, and Böhm-Bawerk often relied on some of the work of the Germans and that all three had considerable respect for Karl Knies. If one side in this dispute had more rancor than the other, it would be the Germans—one only needs to consider how poorly Schmoller treated Menger. The other complaint that some German scholars have was that the Austrians had no use for history. This is a complaint that is not at all borne out by a reading of the works of these three Austrians. Instead, they had a great appreciation of history and each of the three had provided historical accounts in various works. What they were unwilling to do was to offer reverence towards their illustrious predecessors; they believed their duty was to truth and knowledge, and if that meant criticizing the great Adam Smith, then they were obligated to do so.

More recent critics have claimed that the three members of the Early Austrian School shared the same crucial defects and major limitations as some of the later members. Thus, Menger, von Wieser, and Böhm-Bawerk are assumed to have been ardent critics of Marx' economics and fierce opponents of socialism. But this charge is misleading because von Wieser and Böhm-Bawerk were experts in Marxist economics; what they objected to was Marx's political philosophy. While Friedrich von Hayek and Ludwig von Mises were anti-Communists who glorified Western individualism, all three of their predecessors were members of government in one form or another and all three believed in a more equal distribution of money and wealth. Recent thinkers also suggest that the three must have shared the belief in abstract theory and economics by numbers. However, a perusal of the writings of Menger and von Wieser reveal little abstract theorizing and virtually no numbers or equations. Even Böhm-Bawerk's use of numbers is rather limited and he, too, rejected a type of economics that seemed divorced from reality. I would not want to attribute any of these four misguided criticisms to the inclination to pick on a straw man, but I do suggest they stem from either a superficial and careless reading of their "opponents'" works or else a reliance on other, equally, misinformed critics. This leads me to a question about Max Weber.

A Weber Question

It has been assumed that Max Weber was aligned with the members of the German Historical School. He was the student of Karl Knies as well as his successor at Heidelberg. His letters to Gustav Schmoller were respectful, if not even flattering. And, he engaged with the works of other leading members, including Friedrich Knapp and Lujo Brentano. Marianne Weber's mentions of the leading German national economists tended to support this view (Weber 1926: 134, 291, 323, 360, 420). Recent Weber biographies lend credence to this view: Dirk Kaesler's *Max Weber. Preuße, Denker, Muttersohn* and Jürgen Kaube's *Max Weber. Ein Leben Zwischen den Epochen;* even Joachim Radkau painted a mixed portrait of Weber's relationship to the German Historical School—although Weber objected to the conflation of facts and values, he seemed to have approved of the German approach to economics (Kaesler 2014: 640–641, 644–645; Radkau 2005: 506–508; see Kaube 2014). Finally, the scholars who have written the introductions to Weber's works are clearly familiar with some of the works by Menger, von Wieser, and Böhm-Bawerk, his sympathies lay more on the Germans' side (Weber 2017: 11–12) However, Hauke Janssen in the final volume of Weber's lectures claimed that while Weber was not a disciple of Schmoller, he was also no follower of

Menger (Weber 2020: 24). Yet, there is enough evidence that suggests that Weber was more aligned with the Austrian School than he was with the German School. His flattering letters to Schmoller are not an indication of genuine admiration as much as a real understanding of Schmoller's importance in almost all academic matters. But the real key is that Weber was a proponent of theory for all of his life, and much of his criticism was directed at those who devalued theory or simply misused it. Perhaps the best indication of Weber's approach to theory is reflected in the "Exkurs über der staatliche Theorie des Geldes" that is found in the first part of *Wirtschaft und Gesellschaft.* Weber does not disagree with Georg Friedrich Knapp's theory of money; he only notes that it is incomplete.[1] Weber's objection is that it is too theoretical and needed to be more concerned about material factors—which was the same type of criticisms leveled at the early Austrians. This leads me to my final thoughts about Menger, von Wieser, and Böhm-Bawerk.

Why Read the Early Austrians?

In my opinion, there are a number of compelling reasons to read Menger, von Wieser, and Böhm-Bawerk. First, there is the fact that Max Weber not only read their works but incorporated some of their ideas into his own scholarship. There is also the fact that for the first volume of his *Grundriss der Sozialökonomik* he chose von Wieser and Schumpeter to write two of the three theoretical essays (see Adair-Toteff 2021). The fact that Schumpeter later moved beyond his earlier compatriots should not diminish his importance for reading them. It should also not be held against von Wieser that Weber believed that his book-length essay was insufficient; it just substantiates the fact that Weber was always highly critical. This leads to the second reason: Weber's understanding of, and appreciation for, the Early Austrians should help us reevaluate our understanding of the "Methodenstreit." As I have argued, much of the criticisms leveled against Menger, von Wieser, and Böhm-Bawerk are based upon a superficial and incorrect understanding of their ideas. A reading of their texts will help rectify these misguided attacks and pave the way to a more honest appraisal of the "Methodenstreit." These two reasons are primarily historical; but I suggest that there are two, more relevant ones. First, these three scholars were first rate thinkers who were both professors and governmental figures and the conjoined a high degree of thoughtfulness with a cool approach to contemporary problems. Today, it seems that there are few people who are capable of great intellectual ability and have the capacity to act for and with their fellow citizens.

Second, unlike the socialistic leanings of the "Kathedersozialisten" and unlike the radical individualism of the later Austrian members, Menger, von Wieser, and Böhm-Bawerk were convinced that they needed to find the proper balance between the two poles.[2] In a similar vein, they did not venerate history as the Germans did, nor did they disdain it like the later Austrians tended to do. The works of Carl Menger, Friedrich von Wieser, and Eugen Böhm-Bawerk still have much to offer us—and that is why we should read the writings of the Early Austrian School of Economics.

Notes

1 Weber 2013: 416–428. For a detailed account of Weber's discussion of Knapp and his Chartist theory of money, see Adair-Toteff 2022. For Weber's early interest in theory relating to political economy, see his Freiburg and Heidelberg lectures. Weber 2017 and Weber 2020.

2 In his lengthy Introduction to Ludwig von Mises' *Epistemological Problems of Economics,* Jörg Guido Hülsmann maintained that the two most prominent members of the later Austrian School were von Mises and Schumpeter and that von Mises believed that he had the greatest affinity and intellectual debts" for Menger, Böhm-Bawerk, and Max Weber. One has to wonder what these three would have thought about the various ways in which von Mises' own philosophy was a major departure from their own views. Von Mises 2003: xv, xxxviii–xxxix, liv.

References

Adair-Toteff, C. (2021) *Max Weber and the Path from National Economy to Social Economics* Abington: Routledge.

Adair-Toteff, C. (2022) "Weber and Knapp on Money." *Max Weber Studies.* Forthcoming.

Kaesler, D. (2014) *Max Weber. Preuße, Denker, Muttersohn. Eine Biographie.* München: Verlag C.H. Beck.

Kaube, J. (2014) *Max Weber. Ein Leben Zwischen den Epochen.* Berlin: Rowohlt.

Mises, L. von (2003) *Epistemological Problems of Economics.* Translated by George Reisman. Introduction to the Third Edition by Jörg Guido Hülsmann. Third Edition. Auburn, Alabama: Ludwig von Mises Institute.

Radkau, J. (2005) *Max Weber. Die Leidenschaft des Denkens.* München: Carl Hanser Verlag.

Weber, M. (1926) *Max Weber. Ein Lebensbild.* Tübingen: J.C.B. Mohr (Paul Siebeck).

Weber, M. (1994) *Wissenschaft als Beruf 1917/1919. Politik als Beruf 1919.* Herausgegeben von Wolfgang J. Mommsen und Wolfgang Schluchter in Zusammenarbeit mit Birgit Morgenbrod. Tübingen: J.C.B. Mohr (Paul Siebeck). Max Weber Gesamtausgabe. Band I/17.

Weber, M. (2013) *Wissenschaft und Gesellschaft. Soziologie. Unvollendet 1919–1920.* Herausgegeben von Knut Borchardt, Edith Hanke und Wolfgang Schluchter. Tübingen: J.C.B. Mohr (Paul Siebeck). *Max Weber Gesamtausgabe.* Band I/23.

Weber, M. (2017) *Finanzwissenschaft. Vorlesungen 1894–1897.* Herausgegeben von Martin Heilmann in Zusammenarbeit mit Cornelia Meyer-Stoll. Tübingen: J.C.B. Mohr (Paul Siebeck). *Max Weber Gesamtausgabe.* Band III/3.

Weber, M. (2020) *Praktische Nationalökonomie. Vorlesungen 1895–1899.* Herausgegeben von Hauke Janssen in Zusammenarbeit mit Cornelia Meyer-Stoll und Ulrich Rummel. Tübingen: J.C.B. Mohr (Paul Siebeck). *Max Weber Gesamtausgabe.* Band III/.2.

Index

.